The Complete
Sausage Cookbook

Published by
STACKPOLE BOOKS
5067 Ritter Road
Mechanicsburg, PA 17055

Printed in the United States of America

10 9 8 7 6 5 4 3 2 1

First edition

This book refers to countries by their most familiar names.
Please note that these names might change or become out-of-date.

The section on homemade smoke ovens in part 1 was adapted from the section on homemade smoke ovens in chapter 2 of *The Home Book of Smoke-Cooking, Meats, Fish & Game* by Jack Sleight and Raymond Hull (Stackpole Books, 1971).

Sketches of antique sausage-making equipment by the author from instruments in his personal collection.

Library of Congress Cataloging-in-Publication Data

Sleight, Jack.
    The complete sausage cookbook : how to make the world's best bologna, salami, frankfurters, kielbasa, bratwurst, mettwurst, and chorizo / Jack Sleight.
        p.   cm.
    ISBN 0-8117-0336-3
    1. Cookery (Sausages) 2. Cookery, International. I. Title
TX749.5.S28S54   1995
646.6′6—dc20

The Complete Sausage Cookbook

How to Make the World's Best Bologna, Salami, Frankfurters, Kielbasa, Mettwurst, Bratwurst, and Chorizo

Jack Sleight

STACKPOLE
BOOKS

Contents

Introduction

Why a book on sausage? Since my book *Home Book of Smoke-Cooking, Meat, Fish & Game* was published with a short chapter on sausage making, I have had many requests for more sausage information. I believe that this is the most complete book about sausage that has ever been published. I have attempted to put into this book the secrets of the old *wurstmachers*, who are fast disappearing as commercialism forces the small sausage shops out of business.

The making of sausage in one form or another is one of the oldest methods of meat preservation, along with drying and, where possible, freezing. Sausage has been an important meat staple for more than five thousand years.

Each area of the world has its own unique sausage history, depending on the climate and on what meats and seasonings were available. Most sausages have one thing in common: They use meat of one or more kinds. Pork was the meat used in sausages in the earliest written records, but game probably was used before that in areas where pork was unknown, such as the Americas.

This book presents recipes from many parts of the world. It also provides basic directions on sausage making, gives information on equipment and casings, and looks at the history and the many uses of sausage.

I do not believe that one person's lifetime would be long enough to write a comprehensive book or collection of books to cover the story of sausage, but this volume brings a good part of it to you. Happy stuffing!

Part 1
Preparation

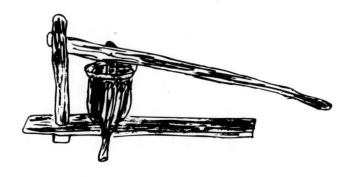

What Is Sausage?

The name "sausage" comes from the Latin word *salsus*, meaning salted or preserved meat. Sausage developed out of the need to preserve meat when there was no refrigeration. Sausage was probably the first "convenience food," predating the TV dinner by many centuries. It has been a familiar product since early civilization.

The first record of sausage is in Homer's *Odyssey*, written in the eighth or ninth century B.C. Sausage is also mentioned by the Chinese and Chaldeans many years before the Christian era.

It became associated with the Lupercalian festivals and, as a result, was condemned by the early Christian church. When Constantine the Great became emperor of Rome and embraced the Christian faith, the eating of sausage was prohibited. This prohibition remained in force throughout the reigns of several emperors, but because of popular protest and illicit trading, it was finally repealed.

During the Middle Ages, practically every nation of Europe manufactured some type of sausage. There is the historic example of the giant sausage of Konigsberg, which in 1558 was carried around the town in procession on the shoulders of the butcher men. Today when sausage is mentioned, most people envision the pork link or patty. This is probably because most other sausages are referred to by specific name, such as frankfurter or hot dog, or Polish, Vienna, or Italian sausage, but basically sausage is any combination of chopped or ground meats blended with seasonings and spices, and sometimes with small amounts of food products, such as cheese, chives, onions, nuts, or wine. The mixture is usually stuffed into a casing or container of animal intestine, stomach, bladder, or a synthetic material, such as cloth. Besides the standard cuts of meat, tails, heads, feet, hocks, trimmings, internal organs, blood, and fat are used in making sausage, puddings, scrapple, and headcheese.

Most sausages are of European origin. Some recipes have developed over the years to be quite complex; others are very simple. Many recipes have become very popular in a particular region or city and thus over the years have adopted that place's name. The warm climate of the Mediterranean, most notably in Italy, influenced the development of the dry or summer sausage, which was made in cooler weather to keep during summer. This type of sausage was preserved by using a great deal of salt and spices, then drying, generally without smoking. Some sausages named for cities of Italy are Romano, Milano, Genoa, and Bologna.

Sausage may be fried, boiled, baked, barbecued, broiled, or used in casseroles or stews. Many sausages have a traditional method of use, serving, or preparation.

TYPES OF SAUSAGE
Sausage is generally classified into six main groups.

Fresh Sausage. Fresh sausage is made from selected cuts of fresh meat not previously cured. Pork is usually the main ingredient, although beef is sometimes used. In some countries, such as Canada and Great Britain, cereal may be added to the ground meat. This category includes fresh pork sausage in bulk, sometimes referred to as fresh country-style pork sausage; patty and link sausage; bratwurst and bockwurst; and Italian-style sausage. Fresh sausage must be kept under refrigeration, and it should be cooked thoroughly before being served. Frying, baking, broiling, and outdoor grilling are favorite cooking methods.

Uncooked Smoked Sausage. Uncooked smoked sausage includes smoked country-style sausage, mettwurst (a fermented type), kielbasa, and Polish and Italian pork sausage. They should be kept under refrigeration and must be cooked before being served. Some varieties of store-bought kielbasa and Polish and Italian sausage are precooked by the manufacturer.

Cooked Sausage. Cooked sausage usually is prepared from fresh uncured meats, although occasionally some cured meats are used. Cooked sausages, which are thoroughly precooked and ready to serve, include cooked salami, kosher salami, liver sausage, blood sausage, and tongued sausage.

Cooked Smoked Sausage. Cooked smoked sausage includes the frankfurter, bologna and berliner, wieners and Vienna-style sausage, thuringer, garlic knoblauch or knackwurst sausage, and German-type mortadella. All of these have been smoked before, during, or after cooking. They may be served cold or heated.

Dry Sausage. Dry sausage is made in dozens of varieties. The two main kinds of dry sausages are salamis and cervelats; both are made in hard and soft styles. Salamis usually are more highly seasoned than cervelats. The amount and kind of spice used in their manufacture and the temperature of processing determine their flavor. Dry sausage products include farmer, holsteiner, goettinger, goteborg, and landjaeger cervelats; allesandri, alpine, arles, German, Kosher, Hungarian, and Italian salamis; frizzes, gothaer cappicola, mortadella, lyons, pepperoni, and some chorizos. They keep indefinitely in a cool place and are ready to serve without cooking.

Cooked Meat Specialties. Other specially prepared meat products, made from cured or uncured meats, are cooked but rarely smoked. These are generally formed into loaves and served cold. They include headcheese, scrapple, honey loaf, pickle loaf, and pimiento loaf.

Equipment

It is not necessary, as is the general conception, to have a lot of expensive equipment to be able to make sausage. Although it is true that many kinds of sausages require quite extensive facilities, many others can be made with nothing more than a household grinder or a sharp knife. Sausage has been made for hundreds of years, and only in recent times have we had the convenience of power equipment.

Sausage-making equipment, in the general sequence of use, consists of knives, scales and measuring devices, pans, grinders, stuffers, and smokers. A source of refrigeration is essential, unless you are using nature's cool weather during the entire operation.

KNIVES
A sharp knife is a necessity. Knives come in various shapes for different functions, such as skinning, boning, slicing, cutting bread,

or dicing. The proper knife will make your work easier, but for sausage making any sharp knife should get the job done.

SCALES AND OTHER MEASURING DEVICES
Some method of weighing the meat and measuring the seasonings must be available, including a bathroom scale or baby scale, and measuring cups and spoons. A scale that measures in ounces or grams, such as a postal scale, would come in handy.

PANS
Large pans or other containers are important for sausage making. You will need both shallow and deep containers, the shallow ones for mixing and aging, and the deep ones for the brining process. You probably already have some suitable containers around, such as refrigerator crispers, large roaster pans, large cake tins, or dishpans. For brining, many sizes of plastic buckets and containers are available commercially. Wood or metal containers should never be used in the brining process. The old crocks are ideal for brining, but because of their weight, I now use plastic buckets almost exclusively. Many of them have handles to facilitate moving around, and they are much easier to put in and out of the refrigerator.

GRINDERS
The grinder is an essential piece of equipment for sausage making, although the name "grinder" is really a misnomer. The cutters in the machine should be very sharp, so that they slice and chop the meat rather than grinding or crushing it. The result should be clean-cut pieces, no matter how small they are. If the meat comes out mashed into pulp, it will not make good sausage.

You should have several different cutting plates for your machine, to achieve various degrees of fineness. Plates with holes $3/8$ inch, $3/16$ inch, and $1/8$ inch (9.52 mm, 4.76 mm, and 3.17 mm) are useful. The $3/16$-inch cutting plate, used alone, will give a medium-coarse texture to the sausage. For a fine-textured sausage, grind with two different plates. On the first cut, use the $3/8$-inch plate; on the second, the $1/8$-inch plate.

For the recipes in this book, if not otherwise specified, grind meat as follows:

Coarse grind: ³/₈-inch plate
Medium grind: ³/₁₆-inch plate
Fine grind: ³/₈-inch plate, followed by ¹/₈-inch plate

To force the meat down into the machine, the safe and sanitary method is to use a cylindrical plunger of wood or plastic called a stomper. Do not use your fingers.

Hand grinders will serve for making small quantities of sausage. For bigger-scale production, there are power models of various sizes, ranging from small ones designed for domestic use up to large commercial grinders.

A handyman can convert a manually operated grinder to power drive with an old motor from a washer or dryer and a little ingenuity. You may have to try a few different sizes of pulleys on the grinder or the motor to get just the right speed.

If the grinder blades get dull, a butcher supply house has the facilities for proper sharpening. A less satisfactory method that can be done at home is to lay the blade flat on a sharpening stone and, keeping the entire blade on the stone, slide it back and forth until the cutting edges are keen.

STUFFERS

Another necessary piece of equipment is a stuffer. A stuffer attachment is available for many household grinders. Larger commercial stuffers are also available, but these are quite expensive. A pastry bag or metal cooking press, fitted with a ¹/₂-inch-diameter nozzle tip, also works well.

A quite inexpensive stuffer may be made from a caulking gun. Have a tinsmith construct a tubular container with a tapered snout that will fit into the caulking gun frame. You can have two made with different snouts to fit the larger and smaller casings. I've even been told of someone using an angel food cake tin turned upside down. Use your imagination. Some early stuffers used in Scandinavia were no more than cow or elk horns.

You should have at least two different sizes of stuffing spouts: a small spout for sheep casings and a large one for larger casings. Although the small spout will work for larger casings, it is much slower, and when stuffing a large casing with coarse-ground sausage or sausage containing fat chunks, olives, pickles, or pimientos, a large spout is a necessity.

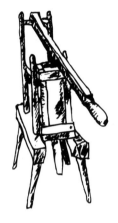

Casings

Both natural and synthetic casings are used in sausage making.

NATURAL CASINGS
Natural casings are made from sheep, pig, and beef intestines, except for weasand, which is prepared from ox esophagus, and bladder. They can be purchased wherever sausage-making equipment is sold. When stuffed, these casings yield a sausage from 1 to 4 inches in diameter. They come in lengths of several feet. The length of gut obtained from an animal depends on breed and maturity. The following measurements are fairly representative, and the ratio of the length of the large to small intestine is about 1:4.

	Length in Feet	
	Small Intestine	Large Intestine
Pig	56	16
Sheep	84	20
Cow	120	30

Sheep and hog casings are available in brine or salted dry. Beef casings are sold only in brine. The sheep or hog casings are generally preferred.

The natural casings are packaged one hank per bag. One hank of size 18/20 stuffs about 40 pounds of sausage, and of size 20/22, 50 pounds.

Natural casings, brined or salted, should be kept refrigerated or frozen. Even in the freezer the brine will not turn to ice, so any amount can be taken out as required.

Hog Casings. Hog casings, or bungs, were at one time used extensively for liver sausage, but in this country they have been replaced by synthetic casings. In the United States and many continental countries, they are split, dried, and sewed to form "sewed bung ends" as containers for cervelat, thuringer, and similar types of sausage.

Sheep Casings. The only portion of sheep gut used for sausage is the small intestine, which extends from the stomach to the cecum. The large intestine is not used for edible purposes. The sheep stomach or forestomach, though not strictly a casing, is used as a container for haggis.

Sheep casings are used for most types of British fresh sausage and for frankfurters, wieners, and bockwurst. They were at one time used for cooked sausage but have now been almost completely replaced by synthetic casings.

Beef Casings. In addition to beef casings obtained from the gut, the weasand from the ox esophagus is used for luncheon types of sausage and Kosher salami, and the bladder for mortadella. Runners (rounds) are used for black puddings, liver sausage, and knackwurst; middles for salami, cervelat, and bologna; and bungs for large salami, veal sausage, large bologna, and as a container for haggis.

SYNTHETIC CASINGS

Edible Plastic Casings. Edible plastic casings range from 18 millimeters to 32 millimeters in size. This material can be kept indefinitely without brining or refrigeration. There is one necessary precaution in stuffing: These casings must be filled from a straight, parallel-sided spout, not from the tapered spout commonly used with natural casings.

Inedible Plastic Casings. Inedible plastic casings, for big sausages, range from 2 to 6 inches in diameter and from 24 to 36 inches in length. They are not satisfactory for home use. As the sausage is smoked and aged, the meat shrinks but the casing does not, so the casing becomes loose fitting and wrinkled. If you use these casings, be sure to tell friends and guests that they are not meant to be eaten.

Cellulose Casings. The use of cellulose casings has increased enormously in recent years. The appearance of cellulose casings is often more appealing and uniform than that of natural casings, making a more appetizing sausage. Since no animal product is used in the making of cellulose casings, they may be used for kosher sausages.

Cellulose casings come in a wide variety of sizes and thicknesses, and have different stretching characteristics. When using these casings, be sure to store them away from heat or steam in a cool, dry environment.

Collagen Casings. The preparation of sausage casings by reconstituting collagen is a modern development. Reconstituted collagen is a protein substance obtained from processed, purified animal tissue. It is taken mainly from hides but also can be extracted from tendons and sinews. This process provides casings of uniform tenderness and good cooking quality.

These casings are used dry, eliminating the need for soaking and flushing. And as no drying is necessary, sausages can be packed or smoked straight from the linker.

Fibrous Casings. Fibrous casings are made of cellulose along with other toughening material. This ensures that the casings will not split when being stuffed, frozen, or cooked. For some large sausages, fibrous casings should be used to provide additional strength. These casings are used for fresh meats as well as cured.

A special type of moisture-proof fibrous casing is used for sausages with high moisture content. This casing ensures that no juices will be lost but are absorbed into the sausage, enhancing its flavor and texture.

Sewed Casings. If you have trouble finding hog and beef bungs for salami and large sausages, you can make sewed casings from beef middles and the second cut of hog bungs. Cut them all into flat strips, and then sew the strips together on a sewing machine. Make the casings about the size of the first cut, extra large hog or beef bungs. Beef middles can easily be sewed and are used in all types of German and Italian salami. Second cut of hog bungs are more tender and require greater care, and they may give you some trouble both in cutting to pattern and in sewing.

Wrapping, or cording, must be done immediately after stuffing the sewed casings. When stuffing by machine, even under low pressure, many sewed casings split at the seams. You can save casings with very small splits by slipping a patch under the cord in the wrapping, but most split casings will have to be discarded. Hand stuffing is by far the best method to use to avoid splits. Save in a clean pan any sausage meat that escapes through a split, or from casings that are being discarded, and mix with the next batch for stuffing.

The finished sausage in sewed casings is as attractive as those in first cut hog bungs. The skin of sewed casings does not peel from the sliced sausage as neatly as other casings, but that is its only shortcoming.

Muslin Casings. For big sausages, the most desirable casing is plain unbleached muslin. To make an 18-inch casing, for a finished sausage about 15 inches long, tear unbleached muslin into 8-by-18-inch strips. Fold in half lengthwise, and press with a medium-hot iron.

The selvage edge of the cloth will form the opening. Near the other end of the folded cloth, make a semicircular mark with a soft pencil, using a cup, tumbler, or other round object of 3$\frac{1}{2}$ inches in diameter as a template. The mark should at no point come nearer than $\frac{1}{4}$ inch to the end of the cloth.

Beginning at the folded edge, sew around the semicircular mark, and continue to sew in a straight line up the torn edge, keeping the stitches at least ¹/₄ inch from the edge. This creates a tube that is open at one end.

Trim around the sewed end and edge with pinking shears. This eliminates loose threads that would adhere to the sausage when the casing is eventually removed. Take care not to pink too close to the stitches, or the casing may burst under the pressure of stuffing. Now turn the casing inside out, and it is ready to use.

If you wish to color the casings, do so before stuffing. Color the empty bags with casing brown mixture, rinse out excess color in hot water, and dry.

It is often desirable to make several different sizes of casings for one batch of sausages. For example, to provide a light snack for three or four people, a 15-inch sausage is too much, so some casings might well be cut 9 or 12 inches in length.

Many smoke ovens have no room to hang sausages longer than 15 inches. When using such an oven, if larger sausages are required, make them thicker. Start with a wider muslin strip, 9 or 10 inches.

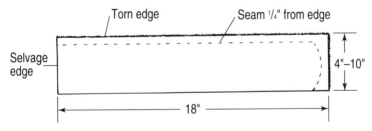

Typical Muslin Casing

Coating Cloth Casings. When using cloth casings, to close the pores and render the bags moisture proof, the stuffed bags should be dipped in a flexine coating. This coating will not peel or crack off and will prevent your sausage from drying or shrinking. Do not use paraffin wax, as it will crack and peel when the sausage is bent in handling.

First, stuff the meat into muslin or linen casings of suitable width and length. If there is printing on the cloth, the ink must not be water soluble. Cook the sausages immediately, for the same time and at the same temperature as sausage in regular casings. Then rinse with hot water, and hang them to dry at room temperature for 6 to 7 hours. Proper drying before coating with flexine is important. If you wish to smoke the sausage, do so before cooking. Hang the sausage in a cool smoke for 2 hours.

In an oblong, galvanized pan long enough to dip the sausages into, add enough flexine so that it is within 6 inches from the top when melted. Heat the coating. When the sausages are cold and the cloth bags are totally dry, dip a stickful of them into the melted coating, keeping the sausages completely immersed for 5 to 10 seconds. Then hold or hang them over the pan until they stop dripping. When the coating is set, dip once more for not longer than 1 or 2 seconds.

Hang the sausages at room temperature for 1 hour before hanging in the cooler. Using this method, the sausage will keep for a comparatively long time without becoming slimy or moldy.

CLEANING NATURAL CASINGS

Natural casings should be thoroughly washed in three changes of water. Make sure the water runs through the casings, and turn them inside out to wash thoroughly again. Then scrape the fat off the outside.

It is often difficult to get casings that have not been properly soaked, slimed, and cleaned white again. Many resort to lime and other harmful methods to bleach them, but the casings still remain dark and unattractive. Nothing can be done to restore yellowish cured casings to white.

Cleaning Beef and Sheep Casings. Clean beef and sheep casings by rinsing and scraping, and chill them in clean water at 45 to 50 degrees for 1 hours. Then apply salt, and spread the casings on racks or tables to drain for 24 to 36 hours. Resalt and pack in clean tiers. Store at a temperature of 42 degrees or less, but not below freezing.

Cleaning Hog Casings. Strip hog casings, and then soak them in 75-degree water for 24 hours. Strip and soak again in water for 3 1/2 hours at 100 degrees F. Strip one more time, and soak for an additional 1 1/2 hours at 100 degrees F. Slime them by hand or machine, and scrape and cut them in water at the same temperature. After grading at 90 degrees, bleach the casings for 24 hours in clean water at 55 degrees. Then salt them thoroughly with fine, dry salt, and let them drain on a table until cured, about 1 week. Resalt with fine salt and pack. Store at 40 to 45 degrees.

PREPARING NATURAL CASINGS BEFORE STUFFING

Before natural casings are stuffed, they should always be soaked in warm water to make them pliable so that they will stretch to their limit when being stuffed and will not burst as easily. Soak the casing in 90-degree water for 1 to 2 hours, depending on how old and dry they are. Old, dry casings will need to be soaked until they are soft and pliable. Do not soak in water that is too hot, as the casings will become scalded and tear or burst when being stuffed or smoked.

COLORING CASINGS

As with any food, the color of your sausage will help determine how appealing they are. Smoking your homemade sausages will improve their color in addition to enhancing their flavor and increasing their quality. But the desired depth of color generally is not obtained by smoking alone; this would require a much longer exposure to dry heat, and the surface of your sausage would shrivel and dry out. To obtain the pleasing color you want, you can use artificial color.

There are several kinds of color enhancers that can be safely used and are certified by the federal government as absolutely pure. One variety will give a rich mahogany color, of any desired depth, to smoked sausages; another will provide liver sausage with its familiar golden cream color.

There are two methods for coloring the casings. One is by coloring the water in which the sausage is cooked; the other is by briefly dipping the smoked, cooked sausage in a stronger solution. Choose the method according to your preference and equipment.

Coloring Sausage in Cooking Water. This method is usually preferable, as it requires no separate operation for coloring the casings.

Dissolve your coloring in a little hot water (not boiling), and then pour this solution into the cooking water. The amount of coloring you use depends on how light or dark you want the finished product to be. You may need to experiment a little to find the proper amount. Use yellow coloring for liver sausage and brown coloring for all others. Agitate until thoroughly mixed. Then cook your sausage for the amount of time called for in the recipe directions, as if you were using plain water. If the sausages are put into the water loose, they must be turned from time to time for even coloring. Small sausages can simply be hung in the cooking water.

Coloring by Dipping. To color sausages by momentary dipping, first hang the smoked, cooked sausages in the smokehouse just long enough to dry the skin well, or hang them in front of a hot fire or in the sun so that the excess moisture will dry out of the casings. Once they are dry, dip the sausages into a casing color solution, using 1 ounce to every 20 gallons of water. Always dissolve the coloring in a little hot water (not boiling), and then pour the solution into the water for dipping. The water for dipping should be about the same temperature as the water in which the sausage is cooked. Dip the sausages momentarily. (Sausage that is smoked only and not cooked must be sprayed with hot water or dipped into hot water to remove the grease from the casings before dipping in the color solution.) After dipping, rinse the sausages with hot water and then with cold water.

Before refrigerating smoked, cooked, and colored sausages, the individual links should be hung apart at room temperature until the surface is dry. This will develop the color and prevent the growth of a slimy mold.

Sausage-Making Instructions

Sausage of superior quality is indeed a wholesome and tasty food, and many varieties are easy to make. Whether you make a few pounds or many, your sausage will always be appetizing if you exercise a little patience and follow the directions carefully.

Weigh or measure all ingredients precisely, or the proportions will vary and affect the taste. It is important to standardize your practice and keep thorough records of such things as meats and seasonings used, grinding texture, curing time, smoking time, and heat used. Then if you are not satisfied with the taste, you can adjust the quantities or methods for the next batch. And if you have not made a particular type of sausage for some time, your records will serve as a reminder.

Here are a few important points to remember when making sausage:

1. Use only fresh meat, and keep it cold before and after sausage making.
2. Keep your equipment clean. When grinding fresh pork, be sure the grinder is sterilized before grinding other foods. Many meat markets will not grind pork for you if they are then going to grind beef for hamburger.
3. Store smoked or fresh sausage in the refrigerator.
4. Cook all smoked or fresh sausage before eating, unless otherwise indicated in the recipe.
5. If making dry sausage that contains pork that will not be cooked, freeze the pork and keep at 0 degrees F for 21 days before using.
6. The amount of water or flour used in a recipe usually depends on the consistency you want and whether you are making links or patties. Add both carefully to the mixture, a little at a time, until the proper consistency is reached.
7. Some of the recipes in this book are for large quantities of sausage. These are intended for hunters who want a practical and satisfying way to use the meat from game they have taken, or for people who butcher their own meat. If you want to make smaller, family-size quantities of these recipes, simply reduce the ingredient amounts by the same percentage.

SELECTION OF MEATS

Good sausage is never made from poor ingredients; the quality of the meats used is critical. The tougher parts of an animal, and some of the other parts, such as lips or stomachs, can be made into good sausage, but they must be fresh and untainted. Before modern refrigeration, spices were used in great quantity to make use of and disguise the taste of tainted foods, mostly meats. Today, however, this is no longer an issue.

There is hardly any portion of the animal carcass that is not usable in some type of sausage. Tough meats can first be ground or cured. Tripe, the stomach lining of the animal, can even be used in sausage and makes a good filler, but it should be ground finer than the other ingredients.

All bones, sinews, blood clots, and tough tissues should be removed from every piece of meat before grinding. These waste portions of the carcass just cannot be ground enough to make good sausage. Don't remove all the fat: A certain amount is necessary to keep the sausage tender and juicy. Without fat, the sausage would be dry and not too tasty. Too much fat, on the other hand, causes poor taste and cooks away.

Sausage is often made from wild game. When butchering, the area of the carcass where the animal was shot should always be discarded, as it is the first place that spoiling begins. It often contains bone splinters, dirt, grass, and other things that come from the body cavity of the animal. This meat will never result in a palatable product.

Whether an animal is harvested in the wild or butchered at home, the last process, after the roasts and steaks are in the freezer, is taking care of the meat for sausage. So it ordinarily is not until a few hours to several days later that sausage making starts. During this period,the trimmings should be kept, at all times, under refrigeration at 40 degrees F or just above freezing. The trimmings may be frozen if the sausage making will be delayed for several days.

CURING AND DRYING

The main objective of curing the meat is to produce a sausage of excellent flavor and attractive color, with reasonable keeping qualities.

In the general concept of curing or preserving, all of the additives contribute to preservation. The term "curing salt," however, specifically refers to sodium or potassium nitrate or nitrite, commonly called saltpeter. Chile and India are the major natural sources of saltpeter, but it can be made artificially as well. This product also adds a distinctive cured color to meat or retains redness in ham, bacon, corned beef, and sausage, including hot dogs.

The methods used for curing and drying sausages vary considerably. The techniques described in this section are the most appropriate to the recipes in this book. Whether you use the pickle, dry, or emulsion cure method, keep in mind the following two points: First, do not coat or wash your sausage casings at any stage during the curing process. And second, keep the drying room at 60 to 65 degrees F with a relative humidity of 70 percent.

Pickle Curing. Pickle curing involves soaking the pieces of meat in a brine for a period of time. With this method, the size of the pieces, their fat content, the brine concentration, and the temperature all introduce a large number of variables. Some of the soluble protein is extracted by the pickle, and this, in conjunction with brine absorption by the meat, adversely affects binding qualities. Thus it is very difficult to control the actual salt content, and often the meat might wind up too salty. This is remedied by mixing one part salted meat with two parts fresh meat for your sausage. In other words, different meats respond differently to the brine, so you may need to experiment with the brine concentration.

Brines. Curative agents are a major factor in successful sausage making. Properly selected brine, seasoning, and cure will enhance the sausage's flavor, improve its texture and appearance, and help prevent spoilage.

Common salt (sodium chloride) is a dominant ingredient in most sausage-making brines and seasonings. A salt content of 5 percent or more checks the growth of most spoilage organisms in meat. Even smaller proportions of salt provide a noticeable preservative effect. Salt may be measured by weight or volume. The standard measuring cup (8 fluid ounces) will hold about 10 ounces by weight of salt. When purchasing salt for your sausage making, try rock salt, dairy salt, coarse salt, household salt, or water softener salt, all of which are perfectly adequate and are much less expensive than table salt.

The water content in fresh meat is much higher than is generally recognized, even if the meat appears dry. When water from the meat mixes with the dry salt or brine, the salt or brine penetrates toward the center. If dry salt is placed on the meat's surface, it immediately begins to dissolve and is quickly absorbed. When brine is used, a similar process takes place.

At 68 degrees F, 100 parts, by weight, of water will dissolve 35.8 parts of salt. This is called a "saturated solution" and is the strongest brine that can be made at that temperature. The strength of brine can be measured with a salinometer. A salinometer, or brineometer, looks like a glass thermometer with an oversize bulb. The salinometer floats with part of its stem above the surface. The point at which the surface intersects the scale shows the strength of the brine as a percentage of saturation level. If you do not have a salinometer, you can make an 80 percent brine by adding salt to the water, stirring to make sure it dissolves, until the solution will just float an egg or a peeled potato. (The potato must be fresh and juicy for proper results.)

A batch of brine may sometimes be saved and reused. Keep in mind that used brine has lost some of its salt content; it should be retested and sufficient fresh salt and a proportionate amount of other ingredients added to bring it up to strength. Used brine will contain bits of the meat that was previously cured and will spoil quickly unless it is kept below 40 degrees F. Even under refrigeration, used brine should not be kept too long. If a used batch of brine shows any sign of mold or scum or develops an unpleasant odor, toss it out immediately.

When meat is removed from a brine bath, certain protein constituents are dissolved in the salt water. When dry, these dissolved proteins form a thin, glossy layer on the surface. This layer, somewhat like a coat of clear varnish, is called the pellicle. It takes on an attractive coloration in the smoke oven and is believed to aid in food preservation.

When using brines, note the following:

1. Brines should always be made and stored in containers of glass, earthenware, or plastic, never metal or wood.
2. Keep all of the meat completely immersed in the brine. If some of the meat floats to the surface, place a plate right-side-up over it, and weight it down if necessary. All parts

of the meat must be freely exposed to the solution for the best curative and flavoring effect.

3. Stir or rearrange the contents of the crock periodically to ensure that they stay well mixed. This is called "overhauling." Overhauling is not necessary if the brining is for only an hour or two. For a prolonged cure that lasts 2 to 3 weeks, the meat should be overhauled every third day.

4. The brine may be kept at room temperature for cures of up to 4 hours if the meat is well chilled before being put in to soak. In very hot weather or in areas where the tap water is warm, keep the brine chilled by hanging a plastic bag full of ice cubes in the crock. When curing for a longer time, the brine should be kept at 35 degrees F and placed under refrigeration throughout the curing process.

Most recipes give the length of brining time as well as rinsing and drying instructions.

Ready-made, packaged sweet pickle cures are available at any store that sells butcher supplies. These are the most commonly used cures. They carry instructions for use on the package. You also can easily make your own. Here is an excellent recipe that will cure up to 100 pounds of meat.

Sweet Pickle Brine for Meat

5 gal. water	5 lbs. salt
1 lb. white sugar	1 oz. saltpeter
6 cloves garlic or 4 tbsp. liquid garlic	4 oz. pickling spices

Add all other ingredients to water. The salinometer reading should be about 60 degrees.

Many cuts of meat too tough for frying or baking can be turned into tender delicacies by sweet pickle curing.

Dry Curing. With dry curing, the meat juices are largely retained, and accurate control over the curing ingredients can be exercised. It was at one time the practice to cure whole trimmings by adding the cure and packing the meat down tightly to exclude air. Small quantities of pickle brine were sometimes added to fill any air spaces in the pack.

Large pieces are cured for 10 to 14 days at a storage temperature of 38 to 40 degrees F. Variation in the size of the pieces tends to produce uneven distribution of the cure, however. The best method is to break down the meat on a mincer and reduce the pieces to a uniform size. A 1-inch plate will produce pieces of an appropriate size. This will tend to equalize the rate of penetration of the cure and greatly reduce the length of curing time.

Thoroughly mix the minced portions with the cure, pack the mass down, and hold for about 4 days at 38 to 40 degrees F, until well cured. Use the same containers as you would for a brine.

Note that pork takes longer to cure than beef because of its higher fat content.

Here are three typical dry cure mixtures for each 100 pounds of meat. Dry Cure No. 1: 3 lbs. salt, 1 lb. sugar, 4 oz. potassium nitrate. Dry Cure No. 2: 3 1/4 lbs. salt, 1 lb. sugar, 3 oz. sodium nitrate. Dry Cure No. 3: 3 lbs. salt, 8 oz. dextrose, 2 oz. sodium nitrate, 1/4 oz. sodium nitrate. *Note:* If pork or veal is being used, reduce the quantity of salt to 2 1/2 pounds per 100 pounds of meat.

Dextrose is corn sugar, and it prevents the sausage color from fading. It does not sweeten food, as does cane sugar.

Emulsion Curing. The American emulsion method, used especially for hot dogs and bologna, consists of deboning a bull or cow while it is still hot and chopping ice water into it at 60 to 90 percent of its weight. It nitrite cure is used, the emulsion will be ready for use the following day. The meat should be used rapidly, and in all dry cure methods, the surface of the meat should be protected from the environment by covering it with parchment or greaseproof paper. In many cases all fresh trimmings are used, and the cure is added to the mass just before stuffing. The sausage is then hung for a time before smoking or cooking, to permit the meat to cure.

GRINDING

One of the mistakes I made in my early days of sausage making was not having the meat cold enough while grinding. I discovered that warm meat, over 38 to 40 degrees F, will mush through the grinder rather than come out in clean-cut pieces. You may cut the meat with a knife at nearly any temperature, but to grind you must keep the meat cold—under 38 degrees F. As the meat goes through the grinder, heat is generated. This is the reason for a 24-hour cooling period before a second grinding. If facilities are available to cool your meat to a temperature in the thirties, both grindings may be done at the same time. Many times ground meat is too dry and warm to put through the grinder a second time. If this is a problem, you may add ice cubes or crushed ice before grinding. This cools the meat, facilitates grinding, and adds the moisture needed for stuffing.

After the last of the meat has been put into the grinder, add some stale bread and grind it up to get all the meat out of the grinder.

For successful grinding, you also need to keep all of your grinding blades sharp. See the Equipment chapter for a discussion of sharpening.

SEASONING

Spices and the blending of flavors are a key to good sausage. In addition to enhancing flavor and smell, spices stimulate the secretion of digestive juices and in some instances provide bacteriostatic and antioxidant properties.

Spices are the prime factor that distinguish one type of sausage from another. The blends of spices and meats are the secrets that were handed down through generations of *wurstmachers* and other sausage makers. Varying the proportions and types of seasonings constitutes the delicately creative area of sausage making.

Spices are either parts of plants, such as the flower, fruit, seed, root, bark, or leaf, or whole herbs that have strong aromatic smells and tastes in the form of ethereal oils. They may be used whole, cracked, or ground. Some are rubbed to break them down;

others are finely milled. Spices should be fresh, as many of them lose their strength if stored for a long period. Should you decide to mix a large quantity of seasonings so that they will be readily at hand when needed, place them in an airtight container and store in a cool, dry place. Even then they begin to lose strength after a while, so do not mix too large a batch.

The meat industry is the biggest single user of spices, black pepper being the most used item. White pepper is used in sausage products where black pepper particles may detract from appearance. Other spices used in sausage include allspice, basil, bay leaves, cardamom, cloves, ginger, mace, nutmeg, mustard, paprika, pimiento, cayenne pepper, caraway, coriander, celery seed, cumin, marjoram, thyme, savory, sage, anise, cinnamon, capsicum, onion, garlic, sesame seed, and fennel seed.

Salt for sausage must be of food-grade quality. Salt (sodium chloride) serves three functions: It dissolves in water to form a brine, which acts to retard microbial growth; it aids in emulsifying the fat in emulsion sausages; and it contributes to flavor.

A few of our common spices come from the following sources:

Root spice: ginger, onion, garlic, celery, horseradish (Schalotten, Kurkuma, Galgant)

Leaf spices and herbs: bayleaf, thyme, parsley, leek, celery leaf, sage, bean-herb, basil, lovage, rosemary, marjoram

Bark spice: cinnamon

Flower spice: clove, saffron, caper

Seed spice: pepper, red peper, caraway, coriander, pimento, cardamom, nutmeg, vanilla, juniper

Commercial establishments use the oils of spices rather than the spices themselves, in order to retain color and eye appeal. Sage, for instance, would tend to darken sausage, whereas the oil of sage would not. These oils are not readily available, however, so they are not called for in this book.

All of the recipes presented here call for appropriate amounts of spices to create tasty, flavorful sausages, but you may experiment with different spices to suit your taste. Your additions, deletions, and quantity changes are what will make your sausage exclusively yours.

STUFFING

Over the past centuries, many ingenious devices have been used to get the sausage mix, also known in the trade as sausage dough or batter, into casings.

The different types of stuffers are discussed in the Equipment chapter. Whatever type of stuffer is used, the sausage meat must be moist enough to be readily squeezed into the casing. Determining how much moisture is needed is learned only by experience and how the meat squeezes through your fingers when it is worked. Some sausages can be firmly stuffed into the casings; others have to be more loosely stuffed. The method of cooking to some extent determines whether it should be firmly or loosely stuffed. The casing can be more tightly stuffed if it will be perforated before cooking to let out the pressure so that it does not burst.

When using cloth casings, be sure to immerse them in water before stuffing. Natural casings should be used as directed in the Casings chapter. Collagen casings should never be moistened but used dry.

The casings can be cut into desired lengths either before or after filling. If the sausage is to be smoked, it is good to have two joined links so that you can drape them over the smoke sticks in your smoker.

Use the following method for stuffing sausage with a grinder attachment:

1. Attach a special sausage stuffer horn to your grinder, removing the cutting plate and knife. Push ground sausage meat through the grinder into the horn until the meat reaches the tip. Slip the open end of the prepared casing length over the outside tip of the horn, and work the entire casing onto the tube until the entire end of the casing is about 1½ inches from the mouth of the tube. The casing will appear all bunched up.
2. Holding the end of the casing in one hand, start the grinder at low speed, pressing sausage mixture into the casing

gently and evenly with a stomper. If an air pocket develops in the casing, pierce lightly with a skewer. As the casing fills, ease it gently away from the mouth of the horn.

3. Twist the casing about three turns to form links at desired lengths, or tie off with heavy thread or light string. If the casing should tear, stop the grinder and tie off the casing; then proceed again.

Stuffing sausages by hand can be done with the help of a funnel, the tip of which is inserted into the open end of the casing. The meat mixture is fed into the wide end, then pressed gently into the casing. Manual sausage-stuffing kits can be purchased.

When making a large sausage such as bologna or salami, great care must be taken in the tying of the twine. Tie the knots on both ends of these sausages like a butterfly, with the twine tied in a crisscross manner. If the sausage is tied with a regular knot, it will slip off as the meat warms, and stuffing will fall out.

SMOKING

Smoking gives sausage a rich-colored sheen and helps retard spoilage. Like curing meat with salt, the practice of wood smoking meat goes back to prehistoric times.

Sausage may be smoked in numerous ways and by various methods, from primitive open fires, hanging in the fireplace or homemade smokehouse, to the numerous smokers on the market today. The old method of firing up the smokehouse consists of building a fire of hardwood in the pit of the smokehouse. This produces the heat and smoke to which the meats hanging in the smokehouse are subjected. Traditionally, the fire was often "smudged" with sawdust to increase the volume of smoke, and sometimes several fires were built in an effort to distribute the heat and smoke uniformly throughout the smokehouse.

Selecting the Wood. First, and this is one point on which all experts agree, no wood from any kind of coniferous tree should ever be used for smoking food. Conifers are the evergreens—firs, pines, spruces, cedars, and similar trees that bear needles instead of leaves. Conifers all contain pitch, which will give the meat a most unpleasant flavor.

The smoke should come from hardwood—wood from a deciduous tree, one that sheds its leaves in winter. (Corncobs, by the way, are as good as most hardwoods for this purpose.)

Some people have exquisitely sensitive taste buds. There are tales, for example, of whiskey tasters who can take a sip of bourbon and tell which county the corn was grown in. To a palate like that, there might be a noticeable difference between a hickory-smoked and an apple-smoked piece of meat, especially if it had been prepared with no seasoning or with only a salt brine.

But this book recommends various well-chosen brines and seasonings. The average palate cannot distinguish between sausages smoked with one kind of wood and another when the food is ready for the table. So there is really no need to fuss about what wood to use. Get any kind of hardwood that is available. But feel free to try different kinds of wood, by all means, and if this or that wood seems more appealing to your tastes, stick with it.

Preparing the Wood. If the fire will be made entirely of hardwood, chop or saw the wood into lengths short enough to go into the firebox. To burn hardwood directly on top of a charcoal fire, cut up the branches quite small.

When using a metal pan on top of a charcoal fire or a hotplate, the best method is to take a hardwood branch and saw thin slices off it—as thin as can be conveniently cut with a saw. Lay a sheet of plastic on the ground so that you can collect the sawdust, too, and use it mixed with the slices in the pan.

Soak the wood in water for 20 to 30 minutes before use, so that it will just smolder and smoke. At no time should it burst into flames. If it flares up, it is too dry.

It is good to accumulate a reserve of hardwood. But do not bring it indoors, where it will become tinder dry. Keep it outside, where it will be rained on from time to time and remain properly damp.

Fresh cut, green hardwood is good. It will smolder nicely. Small twigs and even green leaves can be used as well. They all will produce the right kind of smoke.

Charcoal. Charcoal is now commonly sold in the form of briquets. These are made by pressing powdered charcoal, mixed with some kind of binder, into small, pillow-shaped lumps. They tend to burn longer and more evenly than the raw, unprepared charcoal.

Here is a quick, easy way to start a charcoal fire.

Take a 3-pound coffee can or other can of similar size, and use a can opener to punch some holes around the side of the can close to the bottom.

Get another container with a close-fitting top, such as a 1-pound coffee can with plastic lid or a large-mouth peanut butter jar. Put three or four charcoal briquets in this container and saturate them with fire starter. Close the lid and put the jar down for a while, until the charcoal has absorbed the liquid.

In the bottom of the can with the holes punched in it, insert some crumpled paper. Then dump the liquid-soaked briquets on this paper, light it, and fill the can with briquets.

When the whole mass is burning well, tip it into the smoke oven or barbecue. But use a pair of pliers when doing this; the can will be hot!

This method saves time. Most directions for barbecues say to start the fire 30 to 45 minutes before you begin to cook, but this technique will produce a bed of glowing coals, ready for cooking or smoking, only 5 minutes after the match is struck! Of course, charcoal by itself won't smoke. You need to add hardwood.

HOMEMADE SMOKE OVENS

Here are some ideas for making your own temporary or permanent smoke oven.

Box. A cardboard, wood, or metal box will make a serviceable temporary smoke oven. To use a box as a smoker, dig a fire pit about 2 feet square and 2 feet deep. From the pit, dig a trench about 9 inches deep and wide that runs downwind from the pit. The length of the trench depends on the material of the box. For cardboard, the trench should be at least 3 feet long; for wood, 2 feet; for metal, 1 foot.

Punch small holes in the sides of the box and run sticks or wire through; on these hang or lay the sausages. Punch a few holes in the top of the box for vents; use rocks or bits of wood to vary the

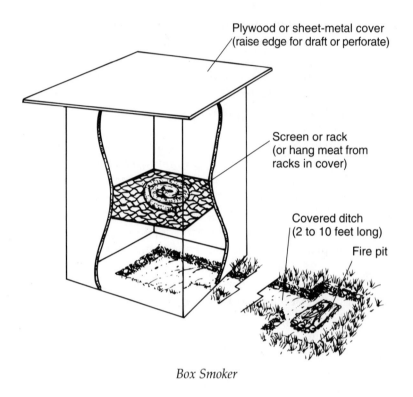

Plywood or sheet-metal cover
(raise edge for draft or perforate)

Screen or rack
(or hang meat from
racks in cover)

Covered ditch
(2 to 10 feet long)

Fire pit

Box Smoker

size of these openings and so control smoke flow and internal temperature.

Place the box over the end of the trench. Cover the top of the trench with boards, metal foil, or branches and dirt to create a tunnel. Between the fire pit and the tunnel, place a damper made from a sheet of metal to control the flow of smoke and hot air into the tunnel.

Light a small hardwood fire in the pit and partly cover the pit so that the wind forces smoke into the tunnel and through the box. Remember that the longer the tunnel, the cooler the smoke will be by the time it reaches the box, and the longer it will take to semi-cure the food.

Folding Plywood Model. A good portable smoke oven can be made of plywood, or even sheet metal. Use a hot plate or a hibachi as a heat source for this model.

The most convenient form for this type of smoker is a rectangular box about two-and-a-half times as high as it is wide. A box 18 inches by 18 inches by 42 inches would be appropriate for use with a hibachi; the sides of the oven must be well clear of the fire container, and there should be a 2-foot clearance between the fire and the top of the oven.

To avoid warping, the plywood should be at least ³/₈-inch thick. Marine plywood is ideal, but a less costly outdoor grade will suffice.

The specific measurements given here are for an oven 18 inches by 18 inches by 42 inches. You can easily adapt the plan to make a larger or smaller model.

The back and two sides are the same size, 18 inches by 42 inches. On the side panels, nail horizontal wooden cleats 1 inch by 1 inch at 18 inches, 24 inches, 30 inches, and 36 inches from the bottom. When the oven is set up, the upper three pairs of cleats support wire screen racks, 18 inches by 18 inches, on which the food is laid; the lowest pair of cleats supports a sheet-metal smoke baffle.

The back and sides are hinged together so that they will fold flat for storage.

The front panel is 20 inches by 40 inches. The extra width allows handholds for panel insertion and removal when the oven is assembled. When this panel is in position, its height leaves a 2-inch gap at the bottom through which air enters to keep the fire going.

A simple way of supporting the front panel is to drill four small holes near its edges. These holes allow the panel to rest on finishing nails that are placed so they protrude half an inch from the front ends of the top and bottom set of cleats.

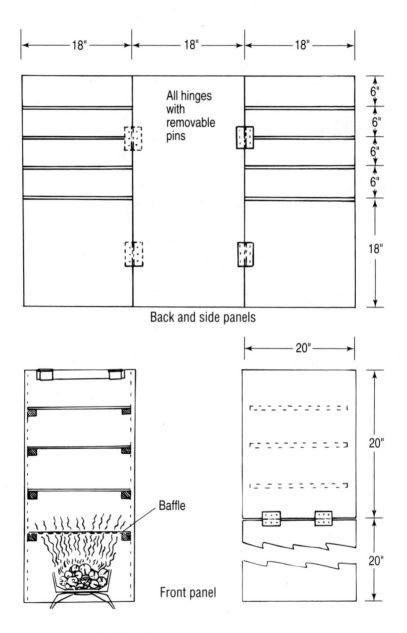

Folding Plywood or Sheet-Metal Smoker

The top is 20 inches by 20 inches. It has three 1-inch-by-1-inch-by-18-inch cleats nailed crosswise to its underside. Hooks for hanging meat can be screwed into the cleats if desired.

If too much smoke leaks out between the joints during use, throw a piece of canvas or an old blanket over the oven.

Shed. A shed can be built or converted for smoking sausage. The best way to use this model is to make a firebox inside—a firebox could be a low wall of unmortared bricks arranged with air spaces in the bottom row, a 5-gallon drum with holes punched in it, or an ordinary barbecue. A firebox offers more control over heat and smoke production than an open fire does. Position a metal baffle over the firebox to prevent the smoke from rising in a narrow stream.

To hang meat near the top of the shed, install 2-inch by 4-inch joists and attach metal hooks. Or, build wooden frames that support removable metal stove racks or sheets of heavy metal mesh. Do not, however, nail the metal racks into place; they must be removable for cleaning.

A vent at the top of the shed is useful, unless the shed already leaks a lot of smoke. Enough air probably leaks in under the door and elsewhere to eliminate the need for an air intake at the bottom.

An electric hot plate can be used as a heat source and smoke generator, but it should be grounded. Run a wire from the plate to a rod stuck into the ground.

Almost any kind of wooden enclosure can serve as a smoker. If no such structure is available, it is not hard to build one. Lumber yards carry plans and lumber lists for sheds of various kinds. You can also use a small prefabricated metal tool shed for your smoking operation. If this shed needs caulking to prevent undue loss of smoke, stuff fiberglass insulation into the cracks.

Remember that when a shed smoker is in operation it looks like the shed is on fire. Let your neighbors know what the shed is used for so they don't call the fire department.

Refrigerator. A good smoke oven can be made from an old

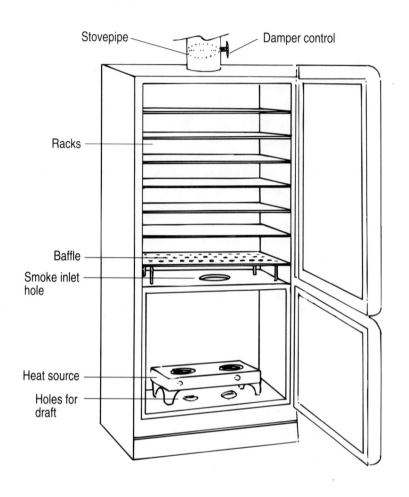

Stovepipe

Damper control

Racks

Baffle

Smoke inlet hole

Heat source

Holes for draft

Pivotal dampers to cover holes in top of unit

Refrigerator Conversion

refrigerator. It is well insulated and so will hold heat, save fuel, and finish off food more quickly than a shed smokehouse would. It might have removable racks and a full-length door that is convenient for loading and unloading.

When converting an old refrigerator, it is best to keep the smoke-making equipment outside the storage compartment. This permits maximum use of the inside capacity for the meat being smoked. Cut a hole about 8 inches in diameter in the floor; 1 inch above it, mount a metal plate as a baffle.

If the refrigerator has machinery underneath the storage compartment, remove it and use the space for making smoke with a hot plate and a pan of hardwood chips. If the bottom section is a vegetable bin, do the same. Or, for maximum capacity, raise the refrigerator on concrete blocks, cut a hole in the bottom, and set the smoke apparatus outside. Build an enclosure of plywood, metal, or concrete blocks around the smoke source so the smoke is forced into the refrigerator.

Cut one 3-inch or two 2-inch holes in the top of the refrigerator. Arrange pivoting metal flaps or bricks to control the aperture of the vents. Or, fit a 2-foot length of stovepipe with a butterfly damper into the holes.

To avoid making other alterations to an old refrigerator, the hotplate and pan of chips can be placed in the main storage compartment. Bear in mind, however, that a refrigerator is not designed to withstand heat. For safety's sake, use only a hot plate as a heat source inside of a refrigerator. With an outside heat source, do not let flames come near the insulation. Whatever smoke-generating system you use, always beware of excessive heat.

To use the cold-smoke process, dig a fire pit as described for the box smoker and lead the smoke into the refrigerator from a distance.

Stove. Although it will have a smaller capacity, an old electric stove can be made into a smoke oven in much the same way as the old refrigerator. Cut holes at the bottom and top of the oven to create a smoke circulation. A hot plate and a pan of hardwood chips make a convenient smoke source.

A stove smoker has two important advantages over a refrigerator. First, it will withstand a lot of heat. Second, if the original heating elements are retained, use of the thermostat or range heat control gives a well-regulated source of supplementary heat (in addition to the smoke source) that facilitates medium and high-temperature smoke cookery.

Barrel. A simple yet highly effective smoke oven can be made from an old steel barrel of about 40 to 50 gallons capacity.

To convert it, cut out the top of the barrel. Trim the cut-out top to make it about 3 inches less in diameter. Drill 1-inch holes through this disk; it can now serve as a baffle. The holes let some smoke and heat through, while the rest rises around the edge of the disk.

The baffle is supported about halfway down the barrel by supports; use stove bolts projecting inside the barrel, iron rods extending across the opening, or right-angle brackets on the barrel's inside walls. No matter which method you use, the baffle should be easily removable.

Cut a firebox door about 8 inches by 10 inches in the side of the barrel, right at the bottom. If it is not right at the bottom, the barrel's lip hinders the removal of ashes and soot. The door should be hinged and fitted with a fastener to keep it shut.

From heavy steel screen, make two circular racks about 1 inch less in diameter than the barrel. The bottom rack should have four upright columns or standards about 8 inches long to support the upper rack. These standards also serve as handles. Fit the top rack with handles made of heavy wire; they must be strong enough to bear the weight not only of the rack but of the load of meat on top of it as well.

The lower rack must not rest directly on the baffle. Put four empty cans or half bricks on the baffle so that the rack is supported 4 to 6 inches above it.

Cut vents in a sheet of metal or plywood and use it as a barrel cover.

For smoke, use an electric hot plate and a tray of wood chips or a natural gas or butane burner. A fire of charcoal or briquets will also work if it is covered with short hardwood boughs to create smoke.

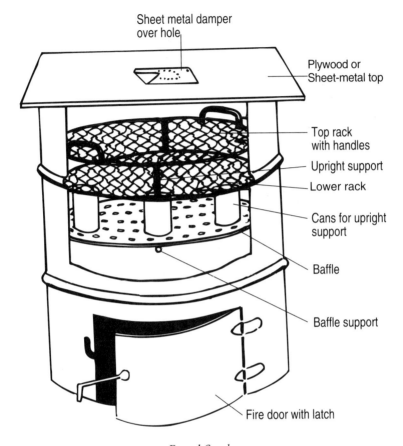

Sheet metal damper over hole

Plywood or Sheet-metal top

Top rack with handles

Upright support

Lower rack

Cans for upright support

Baffle

Baffle support

Fire door with latch

Barrel Smoker

Slightly opening the bottom fire door and varying the aperture of the vents on top gives excellent control of the draft and provides a useful range of temperature and smoke intensity.

To smoke smaller amounts of food, or to operate in less space, make this smoker on a smaller scale by using a 25-gallon, 10-gallon, or even a 5-gallon barrel.

Barrel and box. This smoke oven is built from a steel barrel and a wooden or metal box. In the top of the barrel cut a hole about half the diameter of the barrel. Make a firebox door about 8 inches

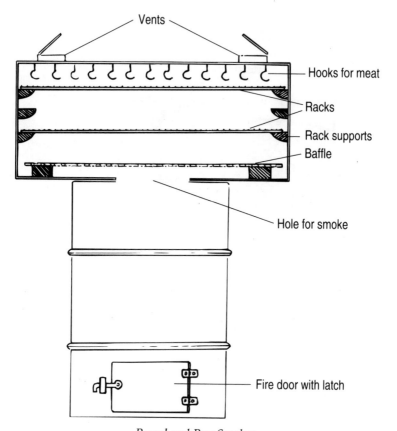

Barrel and Box Smoker

by 10 inches, right at the bottom of the barrel. In the bottom of the box, cut a circular hole the same size as that in the top of the barrel.

From plywood or sheet metal, make a baffle, 1 inch less in length and width than the bottom of the box. Drill 1-inch holes in the baffle and mount it on rocks or small cans about 2 inches above the bottom of the box.

On the sides of the box fasten 1-inch-by-1-inch cleats to support the racks, which should be made of heavy steel screen. In the top of the box, fasten hooks from which sausages can be hung.

The whole front of the box should open on hinges or lift off for easy loading and unloading.

Cut two 2-inch holes in the top of the box, with some mechanism to vary their aperture. If too much smoke leaks out of the box, throw a piece of canvas over top of it.

Masonry. An excellent permanent smoke oven can be made of bricks and mortar or concrete. The simplest type to build is a reproduction of the refrigerator smoker—a tall brick box with a smoke generator at the bottom, a baffle, removable metal racks, and, on top, a brick or metal chimney with a damper.

There should be a door in front of the racks for easy loading and unloading. For this, the oven door from an old cook stove would do. For the bottom door, which gives access to the smoke generator, the firedoor from an old wood-and-coal stove, with its built-in regulator, would be ideal.

To support the racks, embed metal strips between the bricks on opposite sides of the oven, or every other course can have two bricks projecting inward from the wall on each side of the oven.

Remember that because of its great weight, a masonry oven needs a solid foundation.

COMMERCIALLY MADE SMOKE OVENS

Some people have neither the time nor the desire to build a smoke oven at home. For them, several kinds of ready-made smoke ovens are available at hardware and sporting goods stires and through mail-order catalogs. If used properly, these ovens will do first-class smoking.

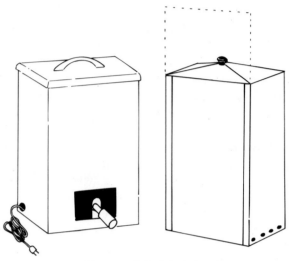

Commercially Made Smokers

TRICHINOSIS

In 1860 F. A. Zenker, a German clinician, pathologist, and epidemiologist, was the first to link the eating of raw pork with an illness marked by the presence of the parasite trichina *(Trichinella spiralis)* larvae in human muscles.

One method of protecting humans from the parasite is by the microscopic examination of each hog slaughtered. Several European countries and Mexico require this or other inspections, such as the microscopic examination of all breeder hogs. These examinations have curbed the threat of trichinosis to humans in those areas.

In the United States we do hot have these stringent controls, and "certified pork" is not readily available. Instead, our pork must be properly prepared to eliminate the risk of trichinosis, through adequate cooking; freezing; or high salt concentration along with time and temperature controls and smoking. You, as a sausage maker, may use whichever of the three methods you deem advisable. From the days of ancient Greece, properly cured and aged sausage seems not to have carried the threat of trichinosis.

Cooking. Pork must reach an internal temperature of at least 137 degrees F (58 degrees C).

Freezing. Meat must not exceed 6 inches in thickness and must be held between –5 and –20 degrees F for an appropriate length of time, as follows:

Temperature	Days
–5 °F (20 °C)	20
–10 °F (–23 °C)	10
–20 °F (–29 °C)	6

Salt Concentration and Smoking. From the time the meat is mixed with the curing agent (salt, sugar, saltpeter, and so on), at least 3 weeks should elapse before the sausage is eaten. During this time, the sausage should always be kept under refrigeration at 40 degrees F or below, except while being smoked.

Storage
Instructions

A ll meats are perishable and should be kept cold. Store sausages as close to 32 degrees F as possible, and no higher than 38 to 40 degrees.

Once the casing of a dry sausage has been cut, place any unused portion under refrigeration. Depending on the holding period, it should keep for about 3 weeks.

When freezing sausage, the storage life depends on the type of sausage and the method used. Do not allow moisture to escape, or "freezer burn" will result. Frozen unseasoned sausage has a storage life of 6 months or more, depending on the method of packaging. Some spices, sage for one, decrease the storage life of sausage. In such cases, it may be preferable to season the meat as it is used in order to extend the life of the meat.

Most sausages also may be canned, following directions in a canning book.

As a general rule, the larger the piece of meat, the longer it will keep in good condition, and the smaller the pieces are cut or minced, the more rapidly the meat will spoil. The larger the piece of meat, however, the longer it takes to cure and to smoke, and with a very large cut, the full smoke flavor may not even penetrate the center.

These two factors should be balanced. If the time for curing and smoking is short, cup the meat into smaller pieces. If there is plenty of time for processing and long storage life is desired, leave it in larger pieces.

Use this principle where necessary to modify the times recommended in the recipes for curing and smoking.

Part 2
Recipes from
Many Lands

Sausages from Around the World

The following definitions will help you identify different varieties of sausages from around the world.

Most sausages are of European origin, and nearly every country is represented. Throughout the world, several hundred types of sausages are made by many processes. Many sausages that are nearly identical are known by different names in different areas.

Allessandri Alpono. American salamis of the Italian type, port and beef seasoned with garlic, pepper, sugar, and sometimes mustard.

Alheira. A fresh sausage from Portugal made of pork, poultry, and sometimes game.

Alpine. A salami type of sausage invented in America.

Andouilles. French sausages made of pork and chitterlings, usually served as hors d'oeuvres.

Andouillettes. Small andouilles.

Appennino. An Italian salami generally put in hog casings and made of coarsely chopped pork and beef with mustard supporting the usual garlic, salt, pepper, and sugar.

Arles or d'Arles. French salami from Provence, very much like Milano, but made of coarsely chopped meat. The sausage is corded in a crisscross fashion.

Augsburgerwurst. A German sausage of lean pork and bacon fat.

Bauernwurst (Farmer's Sausage). A smoked sausage made of coarsely ground pork. It usually is highly seasoned and often contains whole mustard seeds. Resembles a large, fat frankfurter.

Berliner. A smoked sausage made of coarsely ground pork and some mildly cured, finely chopped beef, put into about 3-inch-diameter casings. Dutch berliner contains eggs, onion, bacon, and spices. This is a sandwich sausage.

Bierwurst. See bockwurst.

Biroldo Toscano. Italian blood pudding, a cooked pork sausage with raisins.

Blood and Tongue Sausage. A sausage containing cooked lamb and pork tongue and hog blood.

Blut Schwartemagen. A German sausage of lean pork and blood.

Blutwurst (Blood Sausage). A German sausage of diced cooked fat pork and blood, well seasoned and cooked in the casing.

Blut Zugenwurst. A German sausage of diced solid pork fat, pork tongue, and blood.

Bockwurst. Chubby white sausages flecked with tiny green spots (chives or parsley). Made of beef, veal, and pork, ground very fine, mixed together with eggs, milk, seasonings, parsley, chives or onions, nutmeg, and sometimes lemon juice. Usually made only in the spring. Also called bierwurst.

Boehemian Presky. A cooked, smoked sausage made of cured pork trimmings, flavored with garlic and stuffed in beef casings.

Bologna. A large sausage (4 to 6 inches in diameter) originating in Italy, made of a highly spiced blend of beef, pork, and veal. Also sold in rings of smaller diameter.

Boterhammenworst. Dutch-style sausage of veal and pork, coarsely chopped, cured, and then chopped fine, seasoned with white pepper, ginger, nutmeg, and mace, stuffed in beef casings, smoked, and cooked.

Boudin Blanc (White Pudding). A French sausage made of pork or chicken, pork fat or bacon, bread, milk or cream, sometimes goose liver or truffles, sometimes eggs. Seasonings are delicate and may include nutmeg and thyme.

Boudin Noir (Black Pudding). French blood pudding made of pork, pig's blood, suet or lard, sometimes eggs, cream, onions, spices, and sometimes brandy.

Brackkorv. A Swedish sausage made of beef, pork, bacon, and potatoes, seasoned with sugar, pepper, and allspice. Also called polony.

Bratwurst. A sausage of German origin (Nuremberg) made of veal and pork. Seasonings vary but may include coriander, ginger, mustard, and lemon rind or juice.

Braunschweiger. A smoked liver sausage named for Braunschweig (Brunswick), Germany. Seasoned with coriander, ginger, marjoram, mustard, onion, black pepper, salt, bay leaf, garlic, parsley, and celery. Also called liverwurst.

Braunschweiger Braegenwurst. A brain sausage from Braunschweig.

Braunschweiger Knackwurst. Knackwurst from Braunschweig.

Braunschweiger Leberwurst. See braunschweiger.

Braunschweiger Mettwurst. A spreadable soft sausage made from finely ground pork, mildly cured and smoked.

Butifarra. A Spanish sausage made from fat pork, seasoned with salt, pepper, cloves, nutmeg, and white wine.

Butifarra Catalone. A Spanish-style headcheese seasoned with oregano.

Calabrese. A salami-like all-pork sausage from southern Italy, very hot with hot peppers.

Cambridge-Style Pork Sausage. An English-style sausage of ground lean pork, pork fat, rice, and rusk. Seasonings may include allspice, cayenne, ginger, mace, and mustard.

Caserta. See pepperoni.

Cervelalwurst. A German sausage made of finely chopped pork and beef, mildly seasoned, lightly smoked, semi-dry. Seasonings include mustard, red pepper, salt, sugar, and black pepper.

Cervelas. A Swiss cured and dried sausage made from pork.

Cervelat. Mildly spiced, heavily smoked, medium-dry sausage with tangy flavor.

Chaurice. A highly seasoned Creole pork sausage with thyme, parsley, bay leaves, garlic, chili pepper, cayenne, and a touch of allspice. A relative of chorizo.

Chipolata or Chipollata. A small (sixteen to twenty per pound) fresh pork sausage of Italian origin, typically containing rice and rusk, stuffed in sheep casings. Seasonings vary with chives, coriander, pepper, nutmeg, and thyme.

Chorizo. A sausage of Spanish origin that comes in two types; one can be eaten raw, but the other can only be used in stews. The ones used in stews contain lean beef, lean and fat pork, red peppers, and wild marjoram. The ones eaten raw are made of coarsely chopped lean and fat pork, seasoned with salt and sweet red dried peppers (choriceros), dried, and lightly smoked. Each may also have some garlic.

Chourico. A Portuguese cured sausage made from pork meat and pork fat, seasoned with garlic and paprika.

Cosenza. An Italian sausage distinguished by its spicy seasonings and stubby shape, named for the town near the toe of Italy's boot.

Cotechino or Coteghino. A cured sausage of Italian origin that requires no refrigeration. Sometimes made from pork skins and is usually cooked.

Cotto. A smoked, cooked Italian sausage containing whole peppercorns. (*Cotto* means "cooked" in Italian.)

Cotto Salami. An Italian sausage of pork and beef, highly seasoned with garlic, cooked, and heavily smoked.

Crepinettes. A French specialty. Small, flat pork sausages that are highly seasoned, flavored with brandy, and sometimes contain truffles.

Debrecan. A hard, fat, Hungarian sausage.

Dolc-Salisiccia. See pepperoni.

Embutido de Cordo y Jamon. A Caribbean pork and ham sausage.

Embutido de Pollo. A Caribbean chicken and ham sausage.

Faggots. Smoked, cooked links about 6 inches long; come in pairs. Made of beef, pork, and veal in medium sheep casings or small hog casings, seasoned with cardamom, coriander, ginger, nutmeg, and pepper.

Flaskkorv. A Swedish pork and fat bacon sausage seasoned with pepper and ginger.

Fleishwurst. A bologna-like sausage of German origin that may consist of beef, pork, or both, lightly smoked. This sausage shaped in a ring is known as lyonel or fleischworstring.

Fleskepolse. A Norwegian sausage of veal and fresh pork, seasoned with nutmeg and onions.

Frankfurter. The frankfurter from Frankfurt, Germany, and the wiener from Vienna, Austria, have been so Americanized that any difference there once was no longer exists. The usual combinations of meats that these popular sausages used to contain, such as 60 percent beef and 40 percent pork, or sometimes veal, do not carry any significance anymore. The label has to be read to find the ingredients. All beef, beef and pork, combinations with poultry, and no meat at all are now readily available. Casings may be natural, artificial, or none. The skinless frankfurter is easier to produce and more tender than the others, but possibly not so juicily tempting. Also called wieners or hot dogs.

Frische Leberwurst. A German sausage of pork and pork liver.

Frizzes. A peppery Italian-style sausage made with pork and beef, chopped medium fine, flavored with anise, about 10 to 12 inches long and 3 inches across. Typically wrapped with Italian hemp; blue string means sweet sausage, red string, hot!

Galician Sausage. A cooked, smoked, sausage of Spanish origin made of cured beef and pork, seasoned with garlic and coriander, and stuffed into beef rounds.

Gekochte Schinkenwurst. A German sausage made of beef and coarse lean pork.

Genoa and Lola Salami. A sausage that is usually made of pork but may contain some beef. Generally highly seasoned with garlic. Often made with or aged in wine. Sewed hog casings 3 inches in diameter and 18 inches long are used for stuffing these sausages. A cord is wrapped end to end and around the sausage at regular intervals.

German Sausage. A sausage made of equal parts of beef and pork, cut coarsely, and seasoned with salt, white pepper, garlic, and sugar. The mixture is cured and stuffed into beef middles, about 20 inches long and 3½ inches in diameter, or hog casings, which are smaller. Loops of twine every 2 inches give a scalloped look. Sometimes lightly smoked. Also known as hard salami.

Goteborg. A sausage of Swedish origin made of coarsely chopped pork and beef, combined with curing and seasoning ingredients (thyme and cardamom), stuffed into beef casings, heavily smoked, and air cured.

Gothaer. A medium-hard sausage from Gotha, Germany, made from finely chopped pork.

Gottinger. A specialty of Gottinger, Germany. A high-quality, dry, hard cervelat sausage, pleasingly spiced.

Hamburger Gekochte Mettwurst. A German sausage made of coarse, lean pork.

Haussalami. A Rumanian sausage of pork, beef, and bacon, seasoned with garlic.

Headcheese. A cooked meat specialty product containing small pieces of pork head meat bound together with gelatin.

Hildesheimer Streichleberwurst. A German sausage of pork and pork liver.

Holsteiner. A mildly seasoned, heavily smoked, predominantly beef sausage or an oversized cervelat. Packed in wide beef casings, forming a ring or in 1/2-pound links.

Hot Dog. See frankfurter.

Hungarian Sausage. Similar to Italian salami but milder and may be smoked.

Italian Salami. A chewy, dry sausage of pork flavored with red wine and garlic.

Italian Sausage. Contains cured, coarsely cut fresh pork and finely cut beef seasoned with fennel and wine. It may be sweet or hot (seasoned with peppers).

Kalbsleberwurst. A German sausage made of calf, pork, and pork liver.

Kalbsroulade. A German sausage made of pork, veal, diced pork fat, and pistachios.

Karistysmakkara. A Finnish smoked sausage.

Karlovsak Lukanka. A Bulgarian dry sausage.

Kassler Leberwurst. A German sausage made of diced lean pork and pork liver.

Kayramakkaroh. A Finnish bologna.

Kazy. A Russian sausage made of horse meat.

Kielbasa. A highly seasoned, garlicky sausage of ground pork and beef. Also referred to as Polish sausage.

Knackwurst. A fully cooked, garlicky variation of the frankfurter.

Kosher Salami. An all-beef salami flavored with garlic, mustard, coriander, and nutmeg.

Landjaeger. A black, wrinkly, heavily smoked Swiss member of the cervelat family.

Lebanon Bologna. One of the few sausages developed in the United States—in Lebanon, Pennsylvania. It is coarsely ground, generally all beef but can contain 5 percent pork, heavily smoked, with a sour, tangy taste, and almost black in color.

Leberkase. A finely textured German liver loaf with pork, pork liver, eggs, bacon, and onion.

Leverkorv. Swedish liver sausage.

Leverpolse. A Norwegian liver sausage.

Linguisa or Linguica. A heavily smoked Portuguese sausage of coarsely ground pork, cured in vinegar pickle, seasoned with cinnamon, cumin, garlic, paprika, and red peppers, stuffed in hog casings. Also called longanzina.

Liverwurst. See braunschweiger.

Lola. An all-pork sausage, mildly seasoned with garlic and closely wrapped with twine.

Lombardis Salami. A dry pork and beef sausage from Italy, corded with fine twine.

Longanizo. A dry pork sausage seasoned with vinegar, garlic, pepper, and brown sugar. This sausage is popular in the Philippine Islands.

Longanzina. See linguisa.

Loukanika. A Greek-style sausage made of lamb and pork, flavored with orange, allspice, and whole pepper.

Lunenburg. A pudding made from pork parts and variety meats.

Lyonel. See fleishwurst.

Lyons. From Lyons, France. A fine-textured, all-pork sausage in large casings, cured, air dried, and ready to eat.

Machiaeh Salami. A garlic-flavored cooked beef salami similar to gotto salami, but made without whole peppercorns.

Medisterpolse. A Danish pork sausage.

Medwurst. A semi-dry sausage of beef and pork from Sweden, spiced with coriander, cured, and stuffed in beef casings.

Messina. Sicilian-style sausage of pork, air dried, eaten hot.

Mettwurst. A soft, spreadable sausage, about two-thirds cured beef and one-third cured pork. They are short, stubby, bright red, and seasoned with coriander, pepper, allspice, ginger, and mustard. Also called teewurst.

Metz. A semi-dry sausage of cured lean beef and pork and well-cured bacon, finely chopped, seasoned with pepper and coriander, stuffed in beef casings, air dried, then smoked in a cool smoke. Of French (Lorraine) origin.

Milano. An Italian sausage of the salami type, but chopped finer, sometimes tied tightly with loops of twine at 2-inch intervals, creating scallops. Air dried nine to ten weeks.

Morcilla Asturiana. A form of black pudding or blood sausage. The blood is mixed with pork fat, chopped onion, salt, red pepper, white pepper, and marjoram.

Morcilla Blanca. This is made from chicken, fat bacon, hard-boiled eggs, parsley, salt, and spices.

Mortadella. An Italian sausage made with a combination of finely ground cured pork and beef and cubes of pork fat, delicately spiced with anise, garlic, coriander, peppercorns, sometimes brown sugar, and occasionally pistachio nuts. It is usually stuffed in wide casings like bologna, but it is darker in color because it is smoked and air dried. The fat pork cubes give a mosaic effect when sliced.

Murcela. A dark sausage from Portugal of pork, pork blood, and spices.

Pasterma. A spicy dry sausage of Turkish origin.

Pastrami, Pastroma, Pastirima, or Pastromi. Dry cured, smoked, and cooked lean beef sausage of Italian origin, well peppered and spiced, ready for sandwiches or serving as cold cuts.

Pemmican. A sausage made by American Indians. Lean meat, mostly buffalo or venison, cut into strips, pounded and pressed into cakes, often mixed with wild berries and dried.

Pepperoni, Peperoni, or Pepperone. An Italian sausage of coarsely ground cured pork and beef, highly spiced, and containing coarsely ground black pepper. Usually put in 1½-inch diameter casings, although smaller pepperoni sticks are also sold. Especially good for pizzas. Caserta is a very hot pepperoni. Dolcsalisicca is a sweet one, milder in flavor and packed in shorter, chunkier links.

Perunamakkara. Finnish potato sausage.

Pinkelwurst or Pinkel Pudding. A pork sausage of northern Germany, containing oatmeal. A winter specialty, typically cooked with kale.

Polish Sausage. See kielbasa.

Polony. See brackkorv.

Pork Sausage. Fresh, coarsely ground pork seasoned with sage, nutmeg, and pepper.

Potatiskorv. A Swedish potato sausage containing beef, pork, and potatoes, typically seasoned with ginger, mace, onions, and sage, and stuffed in hog casings.

Redfleischkochwurst. A German sausage of pork fat and beef, seasoned with coriander.

Regensburger. A knackwurst named for Regensburg, Germany. The Bavarian hot dog.

Riisimakkara. A Finnish rice and liver sausage.

Salami. A mixture of cured pork and beef with spices, put in casings, smoked, and air dried.

Salchichon. A Spanish sausage made from fillet of pork, a little fat bacon, and white pepper.

Salchichos. A Sausage of Spanish origin made with a mixture of fillet of veal and pork, with white pepper, nutmeg, and rum. Should be eaten when fresh.

Salsiccie Alla. A Sicilian-type pork sausage, with provolone cheese, parsley, and fennel seeds, stuffed in pork casings.

Sardelky. A spicy Ukrainian, long, thin, hard "hunter's sausage."

Schinkenwurst. A ham sausage.

Schlachtwurst. A German sausage made of three-fourths beef and one-fourth pork.

Scrapple. A Pennsylvania Dutch invention—a thrifty way to use scraps of pork after hogs have been butchered. Along with the scrap pork (head scraps, skin, and liver), ingredients might include, subject to a housewife's taste, cornmeal, salt, onions, ground cloves, thyme, sage, marjoram, and black pepper.

Smedovska Lukanka. A Bulgarian smoked sausage made of pork and beef.

Smyrna or Smyrnaika. A Greek sausage patty simmered in tomato sauce.

Soppressata. A hot, garlicky Italian salami that is smoked to varying degrees and packaged in $1/2$- to $3/4$-pound links.

Souse, Sulz, or Sylta. A jellied, pickled loaf from pork variety meats.

Speck Blutwurst. A German sausage made of solid pork fat, blood, and pork.

Spegepolse. Danish bologna.

Stuttgarter Presskopf. A German sausage made of pork, veal, and beef.

Summer Sausage. Any dry sausage, particularly cervelat. Summer sausages originally were made in the winter to be eaten in the summer because of their ability to stand up without refrigeration. (I do not recommend trying it.)

Suprasodo. A sweet Italian salami.

Svinski Sudzuceta. A Bulgarian pork sausage.

Swiss Sausage. Fresh sausage similar to bockwurst.

Teewurst. See mettwurst.

Thuringer. One of the sausages sometimes called summer sausage. Made of pork and beef, tangy, and mildly seasoned with coriander and whole mustard seeds.

Thuringer Blutwurst. A German sausage made of pork, veal, and beef.

Toulouse. A fat pork sausage seasoned with garlic and white wine, stuffed into small hot casings.

Touristenwurst. A German sausage of three-fourths beef and one-fourth pork.

Truffel Leberwurst. A German sausage made of pork, pork liver, and truffles.

Varmlandskorv. A Swedish sausage made of pork, beef, and potatoes, seasoned with pepper and allspice.

Vienna Sausages. Small cocktail-type sausages.

Weiswurst. Fresh, mildly spiced German sausage made of pork and veal.

Wiener. See frankfurter.

AFRICA

Sausage making is not prevalent in Africa because of the warm temperatures. I did find one appetizing recipe for authentic African sausage.

Boerwors
South African Sausage

3 lbs. lean beef chuck	½ tsp. nutmeg
1 lb. pork shoulder	½ cup vinegar
1 lb. bacon ends and pieces	½ tsp. black pepper
4½ tsp. coriander seeds, toasted and crushed	½ tsp. ground cloves
	4½ tsp. salt

Grind beef, pork, and bacon once through coarse plate of meat grinder. Mix in remaining ingredients. Refrigerate for 3 hours, mixing now and then to let flavor develop. Grind again through medium or fine plate of grinder. Stuff into hog casings, and twist or tie into 4- to 5-inch lengths. Boerwors traditionally are grilled over coals but may also be fried, broiled, or baked in moderate oven for 20 to 30 minutes.

Note: To toast coriander seeds, place whole seeds in a heavy skillet over medium heat. Stir continuously until they begin to smoke. Remove from pan immediately, and grind or crush.

ARGENTINA

Argentina, like all the other South American countries, developed no outstanding sausages. The Spanish chorizos, a type of Italian sausage, are the most popular.

Chorizos
Pork Sausages

2 lbs. ground pork	½ tsp. dried ground
½ lb. pork fat	chili peppers
1 clove garlic, minced	¾ cup chopped onions
2 tsp. salt	¾ tsp. black pepper
2 tsp. Spanish paprika	1 tsp. cumin

Grind all ingredients together in food chopper. Stuff into sausage casings or form into firm sausage shapes or patties, and cook. Makes about 20 sausages.

ARMENIA

Armenian Lamb Sausage

5 lbs. medium-ground lamb
1 cup finely chopped onion
8 cloves garlic, pressed
2 tsp. black pepper
1 tbsp. salt
²/₃ cup fresh mint, chopped
1 cup water

Combine all ingredients, and mix well. Stuff into sheep casings.
Broil or barbecue.

AUSTRIA

Bavarian Bockwurst

3 lbs. fine-ground veal	1½ tbsp. white pepper
2 lbs. fine-ground pork butt	1 tbsp. salt
1½ cups cream	¾ tsp. nutmeg
⅓ cup chopped chives	½ tsp. mace
1 cup grated onion	1 cup water

Combine all ingredients, and mix well. Stuff into hog casings. Simmer 20 minutes and fry.

BELGIUM

Belgian Summer Sausage

5 lbs. lean hamburger	2½ tsp. black pepper, coarse or regular
2½ tsp. mustard seed	
2½ tsp. garlic salt or powder	1 tsp. hickory smoke or
2 tsp. tender-quick salt (Morton's curing salt)	2 tsp. liquid smoke

Mix thoroughly, cover, and refrigerate. Mix once a day for 3 days. On the fourth day, mix and form into 3 rolls, 2 to 3 inches in diameter. Bake at 150 degrees for 8 hours on broiler pan. Cool, wrap, and refrigerate.

BULGARIA

Bulgaria is a Central European country that does not have a great sausage lineage, although sausage is a staple food. Here are some native recipes.

Baked Homemade Sausage

1½ lbs. minced meat	salt	
2 to 3 onions, chopped	black pepper	
2 to 3 tbsp. fat	paprika	
1 tbsp. rice	3 to 4 tbsp. water	

Fry onion in fat. Add minced meat, rice, and seasonings. Fry well. Remove from heat and stir well. Loosely fill 20-inch-long sheet intestine with mixture. Grease baking pan very well; tie sausage at both ends and place in pan. Add water and bake in 400-degree oven for about 40 minutes, basting frequently. Serves 4 to 6.

Knackwurst

5	lbs. lean pork	10	cloves garlic, crushed
3	lbs. beef	1	tbsp. cumin
2	lbs. pork fat	$^5/_8$	tsp. saltpeter
6$^1/_2$	tbsp. salt		

Chop meat and fat with knife, then mix together with your hands.
Spread out on waxed paper and season. Run through fine grinder.
Stuff the casings, and allow to dry for 4 days in a cold place. Smoke
for 4 hours in smokehouse at 100 degrees or less. Cook in boiling
water for 10 minutes before serving.

Pork Sausage

6	lbs. streaky pork
$^1/_3$	cup salt
1$^1/_2$	tbsp. black pepper
1	tbsp. whole allspice
	oregano

Put meat through grinder twice; mix with salt and spices. Fill into
thin pork casings, twisting about every 4 inches so that sausages
can be separated. Hang to dry in an airy place.

Pork Sausage with Garlic

6 lbs. pork	black pepper
1 lb. fat bacon	2 to 3 cloves, ground
3 oz. salt	⅓ cup water
2 heads garlic, separated into cloves and peeled	

Put pork through mincer; cube bacon fine. Mix both with seasonings and water, and fill into thin pork casings, twisting every 6 inches to mark length of individual sausages. Leave to dry in an airy place.

Sausage, Karlovo-Style

8 lbs. pork	7 tsp. sugar
4 lbs. beef	7 tsp. salt
2 lbs. fat bacon	7 tsp. caraway seeds
7 tsp. black pepper	1 tbsp. water (optional)
7 tsp. oregano	

Mince pork and beef in grinder; cube bacon fine. Combine. Add sugar and seasonings and, if necessary, water. Leave mixture in refrigerator overnight, then fill into wide pork or beef casings, twisting every 10 or 11 inches. Tie each twist firmly with thread. Prick each section several times with a needle, and dry in an airy place.

After 2 to 3 days, roll into shape with rolling pin or bottle. When completely dry, wrap in paper and store in wooden cases in sieved wood ashes. Keeps up to 1 year.

Smoked Sausage, Koprivstiza-Style

8 lbs. pork from neck and breast	8 to 10 tbsp. white pepper
4 lbs. beef from leg	8 to 10 tbsp. caraway seeds
3/4 cup salt	3/8 tsp. sugar

Cut meat into small pieces and place in large dish, tilted to allow liquid to run off. Put through grinder (traditionally, meat was beaten with a club). Add seasonings, knead well, and let stand overnight. Next day, fill broad beef casings; twist and tie every 15 inches with a strong thread. Prick each section with a needle so that any air can escape. Hang up to dry in an airy place. After 10 to 15 days, round off with a rolling pin or bottle, then allow to dry for 2½ to 3 months longer. Well-dried sausage keeps for more than a year.

Smoked Sausage, Smedovo-Style

8 lbs. streaky pork	3 tbsp. sugar
4 lbs. beef	2 tbsp. black pepper
5 tbsp. salt	1 tsp. caraway seeds

Cut meat into small pieces; sprinkle with salt and sugar. Leave in tilted bowl for 24 hours so that juice can run off. Mix with pepper and caraway seeds, and fill into wide beef casings. Make sausages 15 inches long, and tie. Prick each section with a needle so that air can escape. Allow to dry. After 3 to 4 days, smoke red-brown. Shape round when they have dried.

Kebabce, Bulgarian-Style
Veal or Lamb Sausages

1 lb. veal or lamb, ground twice
1 onion, minced
  salt
  freshly ground black pepper
1 egg

In mixing bowl, put meat, onion, salt, pepper, and paprika. Blend mixture together with egg, and let rest for 1 hour in a cool place. Wet your hands or dust them with flour. Take small portions of meat (about a tablespoonful each), shape into round balls, then roll into little sausages 2 inches long. These kebabce are best if barbecued or cooked over charcoal heat, but they can be fried in oil in heavy skillet. They are excellent hot as a main course or cold as cocktail hors d'oeuvres. Serves 4 as a main course.

CANADA

Canadian Summer Sausage

66 lbs. ground beef
33 lbs. ground pork
4 lbs. salt

5 lbs. white sugar
⅓ lb. black pepper
2 oz. saltpeter

Mix ingredients and stuff tightly in muslin sacks, 3½ to 4 inches wide and 2 feet long. Hang in cellar for 1 to 2 weeks, and then smoke. Let dry for 6 to 8 weeks.

Canadian Pork Sausage

55 lbs. pork jowls
45 lbs. pork trimmings (80% lean)
10 lbs. ice
3 lbs. corn flour
2 lbs. salt

Grind meats through ³/₈-inch plate, place in chopper with all other ingredients, and chop finely for 1 to 2 minutes. Stuff mixture into animal, cellulose, or collagen casings. Prepare carefully, as this is a fresh pork sausage.

Canadian Breakfast Sausage

50	lbs. jowls or regular trimmings	8	oz. sugar
20	lbs. pork skirts	2	lbs. salt
15	lbs. beef trimmings	4	oz. white pepper
15	lbs. back fat	1	oz. nutmeg
15	lbs. ice	1/2	oz. thyme
4	lbs. corn flour	1/2	oz. sage
4	lbs. dry skim milk	1	oz. mace
		1	oz. ginger

Follow procedure for Canadian Pork Sausage.

Sausage Meat

2	lbs. ground shoulder pork	2	tsp. salt
1/4	lb. ground round steak	1	tsp. black pepper
2 or 3	crushed crackers (optional)	1	tbsp. summer savory
1	tbsp. sugar	2	tsp. sage

Mix all ingredients together with your hands, squeezing through your fingers. Shape into rolls about 2½ inches in diameter, and sprinkle with flour. Chill until firm and well seasoned. Two or three crushed crackers can be added to help hold sausage together.

Homemade Pig's Pudding
Lunenburg Sausage

1 pork heart	2–inch strip of pork belly fat
1 pork liver	2 tbsp. salt
1 pork tongue	2 tbsp. allspice
2 pork kidneys	2 tsp. pepper
pork lights, or lungs	1 cup fresh summer savory
pork fat from entrails	4 large onions

Soak liver, lights, and fat from entrails in salt and water for 1 hour to remove blood. Pour boiling water over tongue, and remove skin. Cut all meats and fat in small pieces, and boil for 1 hour. Place fat from entrails in pan in oven to render fat. (Fat may be used for cooking purposes.) When cooked, cool meat enough to handle, then put it, plus crisp residue from fat (called crackling), through meat grinder. Grind onions, and fry in small amount of fat to brown. Mix meat, onions, and spices well. You may add more spice if desired. Stuff mixture into casings.

THE CARIBBEAN

Embutido de Cerdo y Jamon
Pork and Ham Sausage

¾ lb. pork meat	¼ tsp. nutmeg
¾ lb. cured ham	1 egg, lightly beaten
10 soda crackers (5 oz.), ground	½ tsp. salt

Grind meats through finest blade of meat grinder. Add most of the cracker crumbs and nutmeg. Mix well, and turn out on waxed paper. Shape into roll. On another sheet of waxed paper, spread egg. Roll meat in beaten egg, covering all sides. On third piece of waxed paper, sprinkle additional cracker crumbs. Roll meat in crumbs to coat. Wrap meat in piece of white muslin that has been sprinkled with cracker crumbs, and tie ends securely. Place sausage in boiling water to cover completely, and add salt. The vessel should be rectangular to allow roll to lie straight. Cook for 2 hours, turning after 1 hour and adding more water if necessary. Roll should be submerged during entire cooking period. Remove from water, cool, and remove cloth. Refrigerate until next day. Cut in narrow slices and serve cold. Makes 6 servings.

Embutido de Pollo
Chicken and Ham Sausage

1½ lbs. chicken breasts	¼ tsp. black pepper
½ lb. boiled ham	¾ tsp. salt
¼ lb. chicken livers	¾ cup cracker crumbs
¼ cup water	3 eggs, lightly beaten
¼ tsp. salt	5 tbsp. salt
3 eggs, beaten	4 qts. water
¼ tsp. nutmeg	

Wash and skin chicken breasts, and cut meat from bones. Set aside bones, and grind chicken meat and boiled ham through finest blade of meat grinder. Place chicken livers and ¼ teaspoon salt in ¼ cup water, and boil for 5 minutes. Drain and chop livers. In bowl, mix 3 eggs, nutmeg, pepper, and ¾ teaspoon salt. Add chopped livers. Combine this mixture with ground meat. Add 3 tablespoons of the cracker crumbs. Mix well, and place on sheet of waxed paper. Shape into roll about 2½ inches thick and 12 inches long. Sprinkle with cracker crumbs, dip in lightly beaten eggs, and cover again with crumbs. Spread out on table a white cloth long enough to cover roll, and sprinkle with additional cracker crumbs. Place roll on this cloth, and wrap. Tie ends securely. Cook for 1 hour in boiling stock made from 4 quarts water, 5 tablespoons salt, and the chicken bones. Use a rectangular vessel so that the roll will lie straight. After 30 minutes, turn roll over. Remove from stock, cool, and remove cloth. Refrigerate until next day. Cut in narrow slices, and serve cold. Makes 8 servings.

Note: Truffles may be substituted for chicken livers. Include 1 tablespoon of liquid from can of truffles.

Fiambre Italiano
Cold Pork Sausage

---

1 lb. ground pork	1 tbsp. butter
3 slices French bread ¾ inch thick, fresh or stale, crusts removed	1 tbsp. Worcestershire sauce
1 cup cold milk	2 cups grated Parmesan cheese
1 medium onion	5 eggs, separated

Soak bread in milk, then drain. Using finest blade of meat grinder, grind together pork, onion, and bread. Add butter, Worcestershire sauce, cheese, and egg yolks, and mix well. Beat egg whites until stiff, and fold into mixture. Bake in 5½-by-10½-inch glass dish at 350 degrees for 45 minutes. Remove to platter, cool, and refrigerate. Serve in narrow slices.

Note: No salt is included in this recipe because the Parmesan cheese will provide enough seasoning.

CHILE

Chile Pork Sausage

50 lbs. pork trimmings, cured
$\frac{1}{4}$ lb. Spanish sausage seasoning
$\frac{1}{2}$ oz. garlic compound
$\frac{1}{4}$ lb. chili powder
$\frac{1}{4}$ lb. sugar
flour
cracked ice or ice water

Put meat through $\frac{3}{16}$-inch plate of meat grinder. Mix with power mixer or by hand, adding all other ingredients as you mix, including enough flour to obtain desired consistency. When well mixed, stuff into hog casings and tie with twine in 4-inch links. Give them a cold smoke for 6 to 8 hours, and allow to cool.

CHINA

It is believed that the pig was first domesticated in China, and China may have been the first to use pork in sausage.

Chinese sausage is made from either pork meat or liver; the liver sausage is a darker reddish brown than the pork sausage.

Chinese sausage is cooked by steaming. Place the whole sausage on a dish in a steamer, cover, and steam over boiling water for at least 20 minutes. To serve, cut diagonally into slices about 1/4 inch thick. A traditional way of cooking sausage is to place it on rice while it is cooking. Be sure to perforate the sausage casings. Once the rice has absorbed all the water in the pot, the oil from the sausage seeps down through the rice and flavors it.

Typical Chinese Sausage

20 lbs. dressed pork	1/2 lb. fine salt
10 lbs. clear fat pork	2 tbsp. black pepper
2 tsp. sugar	1 tbsp. sage (optional)

Cut meat into small pieces. Add remaining ingredients, and grind twice. Stuff into pork casings.

Goin Chong

25	lbs. pork trimmings (80% lean)	$^1\!/_2$	lb. sugar
15	lbs. pork back fat	2	oz. soy sauce
10	lbs. pork liver	$^1\!/_2$	oz. cinnamon
1	lb., 4 oz. salt	.062	oz. sodium nitrate

Grind pork trimmings through $^1\!/_2$-inch plate. Chill back fat, and dice into $^1\!/_4$-inch cubes. Pass livers through $^1\!/_8$-inch plate. Mix all ingredients together in mixer. Stuff into size 26 cellulose or equivalent-size animal casings. Link at 4-inch intervals. Heat in smokehouse at 137 degrees for 48 hours with no smoke added. Hold at 60 to 65 degrees for 24 to 48 hours before packaging. These products shrink 30 to 35 percent during processing and storage.

Note: These are essentially raw pork products and, unless made with certified or frozen pork, must be heated to 137 degrees in a smokehouse.

Bok Yu Chong

37 $^1\!/_2$	lbs. pork trimmings (75% lean)	8	oz. sugar
12	lbs. back fat	2	oz. soy sauce
1	lb., 4 oz. salt	$^1\!/_2$	oz. cinnamon
		.125	oz. sodium nitrate

Grind pork trimmings through $^1\!/_2$-inch plate. Chill back fat, and dice into $^1\!/_4$-inch cubes. Mix all ingredients together in mixer. Stuff into size 26 cellulose or equivalent-size animal casings. Link at 4-inch intervals. Heat in smokehouse at 137 degrees for 48 hours with no smoke added. Hold at 60 to 65 degrees for 24 to 48 hours before packaging. (See note under Goin Chong.)

Chinese Sausage (Light)

This is the Chinese sausage commonly seen and sold in the U.S. market.

    37 ½ lbs. lean pork
    12 ½ lbs. fat pork
     6   tbsp. salt
     ¾   cup sugar

Cut lean and fat pork into ½-inch cubes. Add salt and sugar, and mix together. Stuff into pork casings, and tie every 4 to 6 inches. Hang to dry in a cool, well-ventilated place. Should dry in 2 weeks.

   To serve, steam for 30 minutes or boil in small quantity of water for 20 minutes. For quick cooking, cut into thin slices and steam (don't boil).

Cantonese Sausage

    5 lbs. coarse-ground   ¼ cup orange juice
       pork butt   2 tbsp. white vinegar
    1 tbsp. salt   1 cup soy sauce
    ½ cup honey   1 cup rice wine

Combine all ingredients, and mix well. Stuff into hog casings. To cook, fry in peanut oil.

Chinese Sausage

    5 lbs. coarse-ground pork butt
    4 tbsp. salt
    1 cup rice wine
    1/3 cup sugar
    1 cup soy sauce

Combine all ingredients, mix well, and refrigerate for 48 hours. Stuff into hog casings. Tie in 5- to 6-inch links, and dry for 6 to 10 weeks. Cool smoke for 24 hours if desired.

Szechuan Sausage

    5 lbs. coarse-ground   2 tbsp. crushed red
        pork butt   hot pepper
    3 tbsp. salt   1 cup rice wine
    1 tsp. ground ginger   1 cup soy sauce
    2 tbsp. sugar   10 cloves garlic, pressed

Combine all ingredients, mix well, and refrigerate for 48 hours. Stuff into hog casings, and tie into 4-inch links. Dry for 6 to 10 weeks.

CUBA

Cuban Sausage

5 lbs. coarse-ground pork butt	2 tsp. cumin
1½ tbsp. salt	3 tsp. oregano
1 tbsp. black pepper	¼ cup annatto or paprika
8 cloves garlic, pressed	2 cups water

Combine all ingredients, and mix well. Stuff into hog casings.
Barbecue, broil, or fry.

CZECHOSLOVAKIA

It is an old Czech custom to pause and refresh oneself with a sausage or two.

Summer Sausage

25 lbs. cured beef
15 lbs. fat pork
1 oz. mustard seed
¼ oz. coriander
7 oz. black pepper

Grind half of beef with coarse plate and half with fine plate. Grind all of pork with coarse plate. Add spices, and mix both meats together thoroughly for about 30 minutes. Spread out mixture on table in a cold room, so that some of the moisture will evaporate. Turn mixture over from time to time so that all the meat will be cooled. After 3 to 4 days, stuff mixture rather firmly into beef casings. Hang for 2 days so that the meat can absorb all of the spices.

Smoking is optional. To smoke, use cool smoke, not over 70 degrees, for 30 to 48 hours. Smoked summer sausages are best stored in a cold, ventilated room. A little mold does not hurt the quality of this sausage.

DENMARK

Denmark has not yet developed as many sausages as some countries in this part of Europe, but here are a few typical recipes.

Danish Bologna

5 lbs. beef	1 cup milk, scalded and cooled
5 lbs. lean pork	
3 lbs. fresh side pork	2 tsp. saltpeter, diluted in 1/4 cup water
5 lbs. potatoes	
4 1/2 tsp. black pepper	3/4 cup sugar
1/3 cup salt	1/2 tsp. thyme
1 medium onion, minced	3 tsp. allspice

Cut beef and lean pork into small chunks, and alternate grinding through 1/8-inch plate. Cut side pork into 1/4-inch cubes. Grind raw potatoes through 1/8-inch plate. Mix all ingredients together well. Stuff into beef casings, and tie in 15-inch lengths. Place sausages in stone crock or jar, and sprinkle with plenty of salt. Turn every now and then and rub with salt. After 4 days, take them out, wipe clean, put in smokehouse, and smoke at 110 to 120 degrees for 2 to 3 hours, or until they turn a rich orange-brown. Cook in 170-degree water for 40 to 45 minutes, then plunge into cold water for 30 minutes. Refrigerate or freeze.

Leverpolse
Liver Sausage

1½	lbs. liver	½	tsp. black pepper
1	lb. fresh pork	½	tsp. allspice
1	tbsp. grated onion		pinch of thyme
2	tsp. salt		milk

Grind meats fine. Mix well with other ingredients. Fill into pork or small beef casings. Boil 20 minutes in milk.

Medisterpolse
Pork Sausage

4	lbs. lean pork	1	tsp. black pepper
1	lb. side pork	1	tbsp. salt
1	large onion, grated	½	tsp. allspice
1	cup stock	½	tsp. ground cloves

Grind meat three to five times. Add onion and seasonings, and mix well, adding stock a little at a time. Fill into small (lamb, pork, or small beef) casings, not too firmly.

Spegepolse
Danish Bologna

---

5 lbs. fine-ground beef	2 to 3 tbsp. saltpeter
5 lbs. fine-ground lean pork	½ cup grated onion
3 lbs. fat pork, diced small	1 cup milk, scaled
5 lbs. potatoes, grated	and cooled
½ cup salt	1½ tbsp. black pepper
1 cup sugar	1 tbsp. allspice

Mix all ingredients, and knead well. Fill casings very firmly. Place in stone jar, and sprinkle with plenty of salt. Turn occasionally and rub with salt. After 4 days, dry and smoke.

ENGLAND

Black Pudding

16 lbs. blood	2 lbs. salt
8 lbs. flare fat	8 oz. black pepper
1½ lbs. pearl barley	1 oz. celery seed
1¾ lbs. flour	4 oz. ground pimiento
1 lb. rice flour	4 oz. coriander
1¾ lbs. fine oatmeal	4 oz. dry mustard
1 lb. onions	

Blood must be perfectly fresh; strain through muslin to remove "strings." Cook barley in a cloth, allowing for swelling, about 4 hours. Cube flare fat, remove all excess water, and scald in wire basket. Chop onions, and cook lightly. Add to blood the seasonings, flours, oatmeal, and cooked barley, and mix well. Last of all add onions and fat, and mix again. Fill loosely into bullock runners or wide hog casings, distributing fat evenly. Tie off into 1-pound rings, and boil for about 40 minutes at 180 degrees. To test for doneness, prick skin; if no blood oozes out, pudding is finished. Add some black pudding dye to water to ensure an attractive black finish.

Baked Black Pudding

½ gallon pig blood	4 lbs. water
2 lbs. beef suet	3 oz. black pepper
1 lb. pearl barley	½ oz. celery seed
1 lb. rice	1 oz. ground pimiento
½ lb. oatmeal	1 oz. coriander
2 lbs. dry rusk	1 oz. dry mustard

Cook barley and rice in water until well done. Soak rusk and run suet through fine plate of mincer. Add seasonings, and mix all ingredients thoroughly. Fill into shallow, well-greased pans, and cook in moderate oven. Chill, slice, and fry.

Blood Pudding

35 lbs. beef blood	2 lbs. onions
15 lbs. pork skins	1 oz. sugar
5 lbs. pork ears	1 lb., 4 oz. salt
5 lbs. pork hearts	4 oz. black pepper
20 lbs. pork back fat	1 oz. fresh garlic
10 lbs. pork snouts	½ oz. cinnamon
5 lbs. pork weasand meat	2 oz. marjoram
5 lbs. pork stomachs	1 oz. ground cloves
5 lbs. white cornmeal	½ oz. sodium nitrate
10 lbs. dry skim milk	¼ oz. sodium nitrate

Pork parts are obtained from vat-cured pork. Snouts from white pigs are often separated and used in souse or headcheese. Cook cured pork items until tender, then grind through ⅛-inch plate. Scald back fat, and dice into ¼-inch cubes. Place in mixer with all other ingredients, and mix for 6 to 8 minutes. Transfer to stuffer and stuff into size 6 fibrous casings or into ring casings. Cook in water at 160 degrees for 3 hours or until internal temperature of 152 degrees is reached. Cold shower or chill in slush ice. Dry the surface of the product by holding at room temperature, then place in 34- to 36-degree holding cooler.

Note: Blood can be whipped with paddle or bundle of small sticks to remove fibrin. Store defibrinated blood at 36 degrees or lower. Salt used at 2½ pounds per 100 lbs. of blood, together with ¼ ounce sodium nitrate and 1 pound sugar, aids in preservation. An excellent anticoagulant for blood collection can be prepared by dissolving 3 ounces sodium nitrate and 3 ounces salt in 1 quart water. Pour this solution into holding container for blood, and stir gently. Store blood in 32- to 36-degree cooler. If desired, 2 pounds salt and ⅛ ounce sodium nitrite can be added to blood after chilling.

Hog Pudding

7½	lbs. lean pork	4	oz. salt
2½	lbs. pork fat	1¼	oz. white pepper
3	lbs. rusk	¼	oz. thyme
¼	oz. nutmeg	¼	oz. parsley

Place lean pork in bowl chopper, followed by seasonings, fat, and dry rusk. Chop finely, and fill into wide hog casings. Tie sausages in rings. Cook for 25 minutes at 165 degrees.

Yorkshire Polony

7½	lbs. lean pork	1¼	oz. white pepper
3	lbs. pork fat	½	oz. mace
1	lb. rice flour	¼	oz. coriander
1	lb. fine white rusk	¼	oz. nutmeg
3½	oz. salt	⅛	oz. cinnamon

Place lean pork in bowl chopper, followed by seasonings, rice flour, fat, and finally dry rusk. Chop fairly finely, fill into wide hog casings, and tie off into rings. Cook for 25 minutes, then plunge into a salt solution to fix the color.

Potato Sausage

6 lbs. lean beef		4½ oz. salt	
3 lbs. lean pork		1 oz. white pepper	
3 lbs. back fat		1 oz. mace	
7 lbs. potatoes		½ oz. ground ginger	
1 lb. onions		¼ oz. sage	

Clean and boil potatoes, allow to cool, and place through mincer with lean beef and pork. Transfer to bowl chopper, followed by seasonings, onions, and cubed back fat. Do not chop mixture too finely. Fill into narrow hog casings, and link about 10 to the pound. If the sausages are to be kept for any period, substitute dried onion or onion essence for fresh onions.

Pork Sausage

In England, the hog has been held in the highest esteem. During the Anglo-Saxon period, vast herds were tended and watched over, and the hog was a staple food in every family. Hence it was common to bequeath hogs and the land on which they lived.

9 lbs. lean pork	3½ oz. salt
3 lbs. firm pork fat (not flare)	1 oz. white pepper
	¾ oz. mace
3 lbs. stale bread or 2½ lbs. rusk	½ oz. ground ginger
	¼ oz. sage
7 cups water	

Cut bread or rusk into large cubes, and place in water to soak. Also place sausage skin in to soak. Run lean pork and fat through coarse plate of mincer. Squeeze out excess moisture from bread, and thoroughly mix all ingredients together. Run through fine plate of mincer. Remove knife and attach filling nozzle. Thread sausage skins onto nozzle, and squeeze out excess moisture with clean cloth. Fill out and link as desired. Sausages will cook better if they are first hung in a cool place for 24 hours to permit the various ingredients to become integrated.

Country-Style Pork Sausage Patties

In England, country style means that the finished sausage mixture is not pushed into a skin, but shaped into a small patty.

5 lbs. boneless pork fillets or loin, completely lean	2 cups green onions, tops finely chopped, bulbs coarsely chopped
1 lb. white port fat, no rind	2 cups finely chopped watercress leaves
2 to 3 tbsp. coarse crystal or kosher salt	
freshly ground black pepper	$1/4$ cup each other fresh herbs, such as dill,
1 tbsp. caraway seeds	marjoram, rosemary,
$1/2$ cup crumbled dried sage leaves (3 or 4 small packages)	tarragon, thyme, chopped; or 2 tsp. each dried herbs, including
2 cups finely chopped parsley leaves	oregano

Grind lean pork and fat in food processor in batches of about 1 pound each, keeping it all fairly coarse. Run motor about 6 to 8 seconds for each batch, then place into large mixing bowl. Once all is ground, sprinkle with seasonings and herbs. Blend evenly with clean fingers; your fingertips will tell you where there are small pockets of herbs still to be spread around. Then transfer mixture into batches to wooden board, and shape into patties. Wrap each tightly in foil, and store in freezer. Makes 16 servings.

There are several ways these sausages can be served. You can fry until crisp crusted, browned, and cooked through. (There is no need to thaw sausage first; just unwrap and place in a heated, lightly greased pan.) You can add a few patties to a pot of baked beans, or bury one in a small batter pudding for an English toad-in-the-hole. You can cover several patties with brioche or short-crust pastry and bake them into English sausage rolls. Or you can use the pork mixture to stuff a cabbage in the style of Provence.

Veal Sausages

1 lb. lean veal
1 lb. fat bacon
2 tsp. minced sage
   salt
   black pepper

Finely chop veal and bacon. Add seasonings and mix together well. Form into flat cakes. Fry to a nice brown.

Liver Sausage

6 lbs. pork head meat	1 tbsp. white pepper
3 lbs. liver	1/4 tsp. cayenne
1 1/4 lbs. flour	2 tsp. marjoram
6 oz. corn flour	1 tsp. sage
3/4 lb. bread or rusk	1 1/2 tsp. ground pimiento
1 1/2 oz. onion fried in fat	1/4 tsp. mace
2 1/2 lbs. salt	

Cook head until quite tender, and reserve stock. Bleach liver by slicing and soaking in water at 140 degrees. Mix crumbled bread, flour, and corn flour. Add to meat as you chop. Mix in seasonings, and add stock to obtain correct consistency. Mince to a fine paste. Fill into middles or fat ends. Cook 45 minutes in water at 180 degrees, keeping the meat submerged. When done, plunge into cold water to set.

COOKING SAUSAGES

To fry link sausages, first prick with a fork to prevent them from bursting, and put them into a frying pan with a small piece of butter. Cook for 10 to 12 minutes; if they are very large, allow a little more time. Keep moving the pan about, and turn the sausages 3 to 4 times. Serve very hot. They may be served atop a piece of toast. Fry patties slowly until they are browned and thoroughly cooked.

In some parts of England, sausages are boiled and served on toast. Plunge into boiling water and simmer for 10 to 12 minutes.

In warm weather, sausages sometimes sour. To prevent this, put them in the oven for a few minutes with a small piece of butter to keep them moist. When wanted for the table, they will not need to be cooked as long as usual.

Sausage Cakes

1 lb. lean pork	1 tsp. black pepper
¾ lb. fat bacon	1 tsp. minced fresh parsley
½ oz. salt	¼ tsp. nutmeg

Remove from pork all skin, gristle, and bone. Chop meat finely with bacon. Add seasonings and carefully mix together. Pound well in mortar. Form into convenient-size cakes, and flour them. Fry until a nice brown, about 10 minutes. This is a very simple method of making sausage and on trial will prove very good, its great recommendation being that it is so easily made.

Pork Luncheon

14 lbs. English pork	5 1/4 oz. salt
1 lb. farina	1 3/4 oz. white pepper
2 1/2 cups water	1/8 oz. ground ginger
1/2 oz. banda mace	

Use young light-colored pork, with a good proportion of visible fat in the lean. Carefully remove all skin and gristle. Pass meat through plate on mincer, and take to bowl chopper. Add seasonings and farina paste, and chop to a very fine, smooth consistency. Fill into weasands or cellophane casings, smoke with an oak smoke for 3 hours, then cook for 1 hour at 165 degrees. If you want a deeper golden brown color, dip the sausages into a brown dye held at the same temperature as the cooking water. If you want a darker color, add 1/2 ounce of saltpeter to the salt, pass the meat through a plate, and add the cure. Pack down tightly, until meat has an attractive pink color. This curing period will take about 24 hours at 40 degrees.

If you would like a more pronounced smoke flavor, substitute 1 pound of lean bacon for 1 pound of pork. Break the bacon down on the fine plate of the mincer and add fairly early during the chopping, so that the difference in texture of the bacon and pork will not be apparent. Reduce the amount of salt accordingly.

Beef Luncheon

6 lbs. lean beef (cured or mildly salted)	1 cup water
	1 oz. white pepper
2 lbs. fresh back fat	1/4 oz. coriander
4 lbs. soaked bread, pressed fairly dry	1/2 lb. corn flour
	1/4 oz. nutmeg

Proceed generally as for Pork Luncheon, but fill into weasands, smoke for about 2 hours, and cook at 170 degrees for 1 hour. If a smokehouse is not available, include 1/2 ounce of smoke powder in the seasonings.

Ham and Tongue Luncheon

5 lbs. lean pork	2 1/2 cups water
2 lbs. veal	4 oz. salt
1 lb. cooked tongue	1 oz. white pepper
2 lbs. back fat	1/4 oz. mace
2 lbs. boiled rice	1/8 oz. parsley
1 lb. fine dry rusk, soaked	1/8 oz. thyme

Break down veal and pork on mincer. Take to bowl chopper, and add seasonings, rice, soaked rusk, and finally tongue and fat. Continue chopping until the tongue and fat are just discernible in the mix. Fill into either weasands or synthetic casings, and cook at 165 degrees for 1 hour. Dip in hot dye, prepared of 2 parts polony dye to 1 part bismark brown, using 1 ounce of this mixture to 4 gallons of water.

Potted Ham

2 lbs. lean ham
1 lb. ham fat
2 tsp. mace
1/2 nutmeg, grated
1/2 tsp. or more cayenne
    clarified lard

Mince lean ham and fat together, and pound well in mortar. Add seasonings, and put mixture into a deep baking dish. Bake at 320 to 350 degrees for 30 minutes. Then press well into stone jar, fill up jar with clarified lard, cover closely, and paste thick paper over it. If well seasoned, it will keep a long time in winter.

Potted Meat

1 lb. beef for stew
1 pint water
1 onion, sliced
1 1/2 tsp. salt
1/4 tsp. mace
1/4 tsp. dry mustard
    dash cayenne

Wipe meat with damp cloth. Dice into 1-inch cubes, and put into 2- to 3-quart saucepan. Add water, onion, and salt. Cover and simmer until meat is tender, about 1 hour. Remove meat, reserving stock, and cool. Put through meat grinder, and blend well with remaining ingredients, adding just enough stock to moisten and hold meat together. Press firmly into cups or other molds. Cover and store in refrigerator. Makes 4 cups.

English Saveloys

60 lbs. beef trimmings, cured	¼ lb. thyme
20 lbs. hog skins, cured	20 lbs. hog cheek
1 lb. breakfast sausage seasoning	meat, cured
¼ lb. coriander	8 oz. sugar
	flour

Wash salt off skins, and place them in water in a kettle. Cook at 180 degrees for 1½ to 2 hours, until tender. Reserve stock. Run cooked skins through 5/64-inch plate, and beef and cheek meat through ⅛-inch hole. Mix all together well by hand or mixer, adding stock from skins and flour to reach desired consistency. Stuff into hog casings. Tie off in links 4 inches long. After forming eight links, connect the two ends with stout twine, 4 inches apart, for hanging. Prick well with sharp needle. Give them a hot smoke for 2 hours, then cook in water at 155 degrees for 20 to 30 minutes. Hang up the sausages, and rinse with hot water, then cold. Allow to cool for 1 hour, then refrigerate.

Note: In Europe, ½ pound of "B" condimentine is used instead of coriander and thyme.

Minced Ham or Sausage
In Beef Bladders

---

80 lbs. lean pork trimmings, cured

20 lbs. lean beef trimmings, cured

Bull Meat brand flour

1 lb. minced ham seasoning

½ lb. sugar

crushed ice or ice water

Put beef and pork trimmings through ⁵⁄₆₄-inch plate of meat grinder. Add sufficient crushed ice or ice water while grinding to cool the meat and to give it the proper consistency. Add remaining ingredients, and mix for a few minutes by hand or with a mixer. Stuff through a wide horn into beef bladders, skewer the neck, tie under the skewer, and puncture to let out the air. Tie a heavy cord around sausage, first extending it lengthwise from the top down, then under and back on the opposite side, tying as tightly as possible. Then tie lengthwise again, but across the first. Finally, tie around the middle, across these ties.

Instead of cording, minced ham or sausage can be enclosed in wire forms while smoking and cooking. This enhances the appearance, and the sausage will slice in squares.

Place sausage in smokehouse and give a cool smoke, until nice and brown. Cook at 155 degrees for 28 to 30 minutes per pound. (For example, 8-pound pieces should be cooked 4 hours.) When cooked, rinse with boiling water, then submerge 8 to 10 minutes in cold water to prevent shriveling. Allow to cool and dry at least 3 hours at room temperature. Then place in a cooler or refrigerator at 40 to 45 degrees. The minced ham or sausage will be ready to eat the next day.

Minced Ham or Sausage
In Beef Bungs or Bladders

---

30 lbs. pork cheeks or head
    meat, cured
20 lbs. beef trimmings, cured
15 lbs. beef cheek meat, cured
15 lbs. beef tripe trimmings,
    fresh
10 lbs. weasand meat, cured
10 lbs. sweet pickle ham fat,
    in ³/₈-inch cubes

1 lb. minced ham seasoning
¹/₂ lb. sugar
¹/₄ lb. coriander
¹/₄ lb. thyme
1 lb. salt
Bull Meat brand flour
crushed ice or ice water

This is a less expensive version.

Grind pork and all beef except tripe through ¹/₄-inch plate, keeping the two separate. Then put all beef including tripe into silent cutter and run for 1 minute while adding spices, flour, ham fat, and some of the ice or ice water. Add the pork and sufficient crushed ice or ice water to give the mixture the proper consistency, and run cutter a minute longer. Put chopped mixture into stuffer, and stuff tightly into beef bungs or bladders, puncturing to let out the air. Tie double 3-ply twine, and either enclose in wire molds or wrap with 6-ply jute twine as for above recipe, using slip-stitch knots. Make a loop in the wrapping twine for hanging on smoke sticks.

Hold for 24 hours at 36 to 40 degrees, and then hang for an hour or so until dry, in warm smokehouse with a little fire but no smoke. Then smoke for 2 to 3 hours until properly colored.

Cook in water with casing color at 155 degrees for 2 to 4 hours, depending on size. Rinse in boiling water, and submerge in cold water for 8 to 10 minutes to keep sausages smooth and plump. Hang the cooked sausages at room temperature until the casings are dry and the sausages cooled through. Place in cooler.

Oxford Horns

5 lbs. coarse-ground pork butt	1½ tsp. nutmeg
1½ tbsp. sage	4 tsp. salt
1½ tsp. thyme	2 tsp. black pepper
1½ tsp. marjoram	3 eggs
1 whole lemon peel, grated	1 cup water

Combine all ingredients, mix well, and stuff into hog casings. Fry or broil.

Oxford Sausage

2 lbs. fine-ground pork butt	1 tsp. sage
2 lbs. fine-ground veal	1 tsp. savory
1 lb. fine-ground beef chuck	1 tsp. rosemary
½ loaf fresh sourdough bread, torn into crumbs	1 whole nutmeg, grated
1½ peels of grated lemon	4 tsp. salt
1 tsp. thyme	2 tsp. black pepper
	1 cup water
	4 eggs

Combine all ingredients, mix well, and stuff into hog casings. Fry or broil.

FINLAND

Because of the cooler climate, most of the sausages developed in Finland are of the soft varieties. Here are a few favorites.

Karistysmakkara
Smoked Sausages

1 lb. veal, ground 4 times, fine	2 tsp. salt
1 lb. pork, ground 4 times, fine	1½ tsp. sugar
¾ cup scalded milk, cooled	¾ tsp. black pepper
1 lb. ground suet	¾ tsp. allspice
4 medium potatoes, peeled, cooked, mashed	¾ tsp. ground ginger
	3 tbsp. salt
	2 tbsp. brown sugar
	water

Combine veal, pork, milk, suet, potatoes, 2 teaspoons salt, sugar, pepper, allspice, and ginger into a smooth mixture. Add enough water (about 2 cups) so that mixture is soft enough to press into sausage casings (somewhat softer than a meat loaf mixture). Cut sausage casings in 7-inch strips, and knot an end of each. Press mixture through cookie press, sausage press, or pastry bag into prepared casings, making individual sausages. Pack very well into casings, and knot the other end. Mix 2 tablespoons salt and brown sugar, and rub over sausages. Put sausages into bowl or pan, cover with cold water, and let stand overnight in the refrigerator. Smoke the sausages over very low coals in a covered barbecue for 4 to 6 hours (or in a smokehouse for 2 to 3 days). Makes about 4 pounds of sausages.

Slice thinly for an open-faced sandwich topping or brown in butter as a main course. Serve with Finnish-style mustard.

Kestomakkara
Meat Sausage

---

2 lbs. lean ground beef	1/4 cup beer, cognac,
3/4 lb. lean ground pork	or brandy
3 tsp. salt	1 lb. side pork, unsalted,
1 tsp. black pepper	cut in 1/4-inch cubes
1 tsp. allspice	1 1/2 tbsp. salt
1/4 tsp. ground cloves	1 tbsp. sugar
1 tsp. sugar	1 tsp. saltpeter (optional)

Combine beef, ground pork, salt, pepper, allspice, cloves, 1 teaspoon sugar, and beer, cognac, or brandy; mix thoroughly. Knead until very smooth. Add side pork, kneading it in very well. If mixture seems dry, add water until it is the consistency of a meat loaf mixture. Put mixture into sausage press, pastry bag, or large cookie press, and press into sausage casings, packing it in well, so that there are no air bubbles. Tie in 4-inch lengths with string.

Rub sausages with a mixture of 1 1/2 tablespoons salt, 1 tablespoon sugar, and 1 teaspoon saltpeter. Cover and refrigerate for 2 days, turning sausages as a brine collects in the pan. Remove from brine, rinse, and smoke in meat smokehouse or over very low coals on covered barbecue for 3 to 4 hours, adding dampened hickory chips to fire, which should be low so that sausages neither break nor burn. Refrigerate, freeze, or serve immediately. Slice to serve. Makes about 4 pounds of sausage.

Perunamakkara
Potato Sausage

This is the most popular of the homemade Finnish sausages. It has a mildly spicy flavor and soft texture.

2 lbs. ground lean pork	1 tsp. ground ginger
1 lb. ground lean beef	3 tsp. salt
2 large potatoes, peeled, cooked, mashed	1/4 tsp. nutmeg additional salt
4 cups milk	

Combine pork, beef, and potatoes, and mix thoroughly. Mix in milk, ginger, 3 teaspoons salt, and nutmeg. Beat very well until mixture is thick and smooth. Press through large pastry bag, cookie press, or sausage press into casings. Fill casings loosely so that meat has room to expand while cooking. Casings shrink quickly when boiling water is poured over them, and they will burst if filled too full. Tie in 6-inch lengths with string. Sprinkle sausages lightly with additional salt, and let stand in refrigerator overnight. Store in saltwater brine (3 tablespoons salt per quart of water) or freeze.

To serve, simmer in water to cover, cook in a soup, or bake in the oven until browned. Prick with a needle in several places while cooking to allow air bubbles to escape and to keep sausages from bursting. Serve hot. Makes about 5 pounds of sausages.

Riisimakkara
Rice and Liver Sausage

---

³/₄ lb. liver, sliced	1 cup raisins (optional)
1 medium onion, minced	¹/₄ cup dark corn syrup
¹/₄ cup butter	¹/₄ tsp. ground ginger
2 cups cooked rice, chilled	¹/₂ tsp. white pepper
2 eggs, slightly beaten	3 tsp. salt
¹/₂ cup milk	

Put liver through finest blade of meat chopper (easiest to do when liver is partially frozen). Brown liver and onion in butter until redness disappears from liver, and onion is cooked. Turn into mixing bowl, and add rice, eggs, milk, raisins, corn syrup, ginger, pepper, and salt. The mixture will be very thin. Put mixture into sausage press, pastry bag, or cookie press, and press into prepared sausage casings. Fill casings very loosely, for they shrink quickly when cooked, and they will burst if filled too full. Tie sausages into 6-inch lengths, leaving plenty of room for casings to shrink. Put into large pot in one layer, and add boiling water to cover. Prick sausages with a pin or needle to let the air escape. Simmer (do not boil) for 30 minutes, occasionally pricking the sausage. Drain and cool. Store in refrigerator or freezer. To serve, bake in warm oven or brown in butter in frying pan until heated through. Makes about 1¹/₂ pounds of sausages.

FRANCE

France is the country for fresh sausage, still an honorable form of nourishment and pleasure, and produced by thousands of chair-cutiers. Although the meat is basically pork, from neck and shoulders and sowbelly, a resourceful use of seasonings and other ingredients produces a variety of tasty sausages.

French Country Beef Sausage

4 lbs. lean beef	2 tbsp. chopped pimiento
2 lbs. lean bacon	2½ tbsp. salt
1 cup water	3 tsp. freshly ground
4 cloves garlic, pressed	black pepper

Grind beef with fine plate, along with bacon. Mix well with other ingredients, and stuff into sheep casings. Tie every 4 to 6 inches, and smoke very lightly. Poach in water for 10 to 12 minutes.

Chair à Saucisse
Sausage Meat

1 lb. lean pork from
   neck or shoulder
½ lb. hard fat back
	½ tsp. quatre-épices
	   black pepper
	2 tbsp. salt

OR

1 lb. lean pork from
   neck or shoulder
1 lb. hard fat back
   plenty of sage, parsley,
   or thyme
	2 rounded tbsp. salt
	   black pepper
	1 tsp. cinnamon

OR

½ lb. lean pork from neck
   or shoulder
½ lb. hard fat back or
   bacon fat
	½ lb. veal
	   seasonings as desired

OR

½ lb. poultry or game ¼ lb. lean pork ¼ lb. veal	½ lb. hard fat back seasonings as desired

Put meat ingredients through grinder once or twice, according to the texture desired. Add seasonings, and mix thoroughly. To any of the above recipes, you can add ¼ cup brandy or ⅓ to ⅔ cup bread crumbs if desired.

Note: If you want to bind these sausage meats for stuffing a bird or making a paté, add 1 egg, 2 tablespoons salt, and 1 teaspoon spices for each pound of meat (lean and fat).

Quatre-épices consists of seven parts of white pepper mixed with one part each of cloves, cinnamon, ginger, and ground nutmeg.

SAUSAGE WITHOUT SKINS

Crepinettes

To make crepinettes, use one of the previous sausage meat recipes, plus a piece of caul fat for wrapping. Caul fat is stiff and is easily torn if you try to pull it out. Soak it in a little tepid water with 1 tablespoon of vinegar while you prepare the mixture. Once it has become pliable, it is easily cut into rough 4- or 5-inch squares with a pair of kitchen scissors. Lay one of the squares over your hand, put a lump of sausage meat in the middle, and wrap it up, overlapping the edges neatly. The conventional shape is a flattish, rather round-angled triangle or oval about ½ inch thick. Continue until you have used all the mixture.

Crepinettes aux Pistaches
Crepinettes with Pistachios

For each pound of sausage meat, add 2 to 3 ounces of blanched, chopped pistachio nuts.

Crepinettes aux Marrons
Crepinettes with Chestnuts

For each pound of sausage meat, add ¼ pound of roughly chopped chestnuts—not too fine, or you will lose the mealy chestnut texture. To prepare chestnuts, slash, put on baking tray, and place in hot oven for 10 minutes before shelling them.

Crepinettes aux Cumin
Crepinettes with Cumin

For each pound of sausage meat, add 1 red pepper that has been seeded, blanched for 5 minutes in boiling water, and roughly chopped; 2 cloves of garlic, crushed; and 2 ounces of cumin seeds.

Crepinettes de Foie
Liver Crepinettes

This recipe can be made from the livers of chicken or other poultry or wildfowl. The heart could be added too. Weigh the liver and heart.

⅛ lb. chicken livers	1 small egg
³⁄₁₆ lb. fresh hard fat back or ham fat parsley or a dash of Madeira or brandy	2 tbsp. thick white sauce salt fine white pepper white bread crumbs
¼ lb. finest fresh pork tenderloin or mild ham	squares of caul fat truffle parings (optional)

Grind meats well. Beat egg, and add not quite all of it to meat, along with white sauce. Season with salt, pepper, and parsley or alcohol, and wrap in squares of caul fat. If you have some truffle parings, add them in a central sandwiched layer surrounded by the sausage. Brush crepinettes with remaining beaten egg, roll in white bread crumbs, and gently fry in butter.

You can also put this mixture into sausage skins, but do not fry. Leave them for 2 days in a cool, dry place, then simmer for 45 minutes in stock or water. Prick with a needle as they rise to the surface. Eat them cold.

Gayettes de Provence

1	lb. pork liver	salt
¼	lb. lean pork from neck or shoulder	black pepper
		seasonings as desired
¼	lb. hard fat back	2 cloves garlic, crushed
	plenty of parsley or other herb, chopped	lard or butter
		squares of caul fat

Grind meats, add seasonings, and wrap in pieces of caul fat as for crepinettes, but form more in the shape of small, round dumplings. Lay them close together in greased baking dish; the oval yellow and brown French gratin dishes are ideal. Melt a little lard or butter and pour over. Bake for 40 minutes at 350 degrees.

Gayettes

Here is a more economical way to make Gayettes de Provence.

From the chaircutier's point of view, gayettes are a way of using up the pig's lungs and spleen. You can also use a mixture of liver, lungs, and spleen, with more liver than anything else. Cut off all the gristly bits, and weigh the results. Add one third of the weight in sausage meat (half lean, half fat pork), and follow procedure for Gayettes de Provence.

SAUCISSES (SMALLER SAUSAGES)

Saucisses de Campagne
Country Sausages

These country sausages are very good in cassoulets or in thick cabbage soups (potées or garbures), which are very popular in the French countryside in winter.

1 lb. lean pork from neck or shoulder	¼ cup red wine / good pinch of saltpeter
½ lb. hard fat back	¼ tsp. sugar
¼ tsp. black pepper	2 tbsp. salt
¼ tsp. quatre-épices	

Grind meats, not too finely, and add wine, saltpeter, and seasonings. Beef intestines ideally should be used for the skins, but you may make do with sheep guts. Use the widest sausage skins possible. Fill skins, twisting them every 6 to 8 inches. Hang them in a dry, airy place (60 degrees) for 3 days, 2 days in warmer temperatures. Once dried, they will keep in a very cool place for several weeks.

If you want to vary the seasonings, you can add any of the following: savory, tarragon, garlic, thyme, wild thyme, chives, bay leaves, coriander, sweet marjoram, shallots, crushed juniper berries, parsley, pimiento, or sage.

Saucisses de Toulouse

1½ lbs. lean pork from
    neck or shoulder
½ lb. hard fat back
2 tbsp. salt

2 scant tbsp. sugar
pinch white pepper
pinch saltpeter

The distinguishing characteristic of this sausage is its coarsely chopped meat—do not grind, as this would make mixture too fine. Mix in seasonings, and leave overnight in dish with lid. The next day, stir ingredients well and fill skins, using very large-holed plate of electric grinder with sausage-making attachment. Sausages are ready to use but improve after a day or two.

Saucisses au Foie de Porc
Pork Liver Sausages

This is a heavy sausage, much like black pudding.

1 lb. pork liver
1 lb. leg of pork, salted in
    brine for 3 days
1 lb. hard fat back
½ lb. (3 medium) onions
    chopped and cooked in butter

2 heaping tbsp. salt
1 tsp. black pepper
¼ tsp. quatre-épices
¼ cup Kirsch

Grind liver two or three times, until you get a virtual puree. Put lean and fat pork twice through grinder, and mix with liver. Reduce cooked onions to a mash, then add to meats with other seasonings and Kirsch. Mix well. Stuff into casings and hang in a cool, airy place for 2 days, then poach in very hot but not boiling water for 1 hour. Prick with a needle as they rise to the surface. Drain well and cool.

Saucisses d'Alsace-Lorraine
Christmas Sausages

2 lbs. lean pork shoulder	2 heaping tbsp. salt
1 lb. hard fat back	½ tsp. black pepper
½ tsp. sugar	½ tsp. quatre-épices
good pinch saltpeter	

Grind meat and fat, and add seasonings. Fill skins, and twist sausages into 4-inch lengths. These are Christmastime sausages, and the chains are tied together at each end to form a circle. Hang from a hook in an airy place (60 degrees) for 24 hours to dry. The festive tradition calls for brushing a third of them with caramelized sugar or red food coloring and wrapping the rest in silver and gold foil. Hang them on the Christmas tree on Christmas Eve.

Saucisses de Perigord
Elegant Festival Sausages

1 lb. lean pork	½ tsp. sugar
¾ lb. hard fat back	1 tbsp. salt
¼ cup dry white wine	½ tsp. black pepper
up to 2 oz. truffles	½ tsp. quatre-épices

Grind meat and fat, mix in remaining ingredients, and stir well. Leave in a covered dish for a day so that the flavors blend together well, then fill skins.

Saucisses au Champagne
Sausages with Champagne

This sausage is, according to the French chaircutier, the finest of them all. It should be made from the still-warm, freshly killed pig so that the champagne will be readily absorbed. You must scald the grinder and basin, too, so that they will not chill the meat before you add the champagne.

1½ lbs. lean meat, shoulder or leg	3 eggs, fresh laid, if possible
1½ lbs. hard fat back	½ bottle champagne
2 heaping tbsp. salt	5 oz. truffles
1 tsp. white pepper	chipolata skins
1 tsp. quatre-épices	

Grind meat and fat finely, two or three times. Mix in seasonings, butter, and eggs, then stir in champagne gradually. Finally add truffles. Put into chipolata skins, twisting every 6 inches. Leave in a cool place, not a refrigerator, for 2 days to mature.

Saucisses Espagnoles
Spanish Sausages

1 lb. lean pork	2 tbsp. salt
1 lb. hard fat back	1 tsp. quatre-épices
½ small red pepper, crushed, or ½ tsp. cayenne	¼ cup raisins, chopped

Grind meat and fat, and add seasonings and raisins. Fill skins, twisting every 4 to 5 inches, and smoke lightly.

Saucisses Viennoises
Vienna Sausages

1 lb. lean pork	½ tsp. cayenne
½ lb. veal	½ tsp. coriander
½ lb. fillet steak	½ tsp. saltpeter
2 tbsp. salt	2 cups warm water

Grind meats as finely as possible—at least twice through the machine. Add seasonings and warm water, stirring in bit by bit. Fill wide, 1-inch-diameter, sausage skins, smoke quickly, and simmer for 10 minutes in water just on the boil. Prick sausages with a fine needle as they rise to the surface.

Saucisses Allemandes (d'Augsbourg)
German Sausages

2 lbs. lean pork from neck	½ tsp. black pepper
½ lb. hard fat back or bacon	2 tbsp. salt
1 tsp. quatre-épices, or mixed cinnamon, nutmeg, and cloves	good pinch of saltpeter

Grind pork coarsely, season it, and add fat back or bacon cut in very small dice—⅛ to ¼ inch. Fill skins, and dry in an airy place at about 60 degrees for 4 days. Smoke sausages lightly and quickly, then simmer for 15 to 30 minutes, according to thickness of sausage.

Saucisses au Cumin (Croquantes)
Sausages with Cumin

These sausages are popular in northern France. The cumin-flavored sausages are known as knackwurst in Germany.

1½ lbs. lean pork from shoulder or neck	4 rounded tbsp. salt
1 lb. lean beef	1 tsp. black pepper
½ lb. hard fat back	2 tsp. chopped red pepper
scant tsp. saltpeter	2 oz. cumin seeds, crushed
2 large cloves crushed to pulo with a little salt	1 cup water

Grind beef very finely, and season with a little saltpeter. Then grind lean and fat pork, not quite as finely. Mix everything together with electric beater, and slowly add water while stirring.

Fill the skins, twisting every 4 to 5 inches. Dry in an airy place (60 degrees) for 2 to 5 days, according to the humidity, then smoke for 2 days. Store in a cool place.

Saucisses de Francfort (or de Strasbourg)

1½ lbs. shoulder and leg of pork, salted in brine for 3 days if possible
1 lb. hard fat back
2 tbsp. salt
1 tsp. white pepper

1 scant tsp. mace, or nutmeg and cinnamon mixed
1 tsp. coriander
tiny pinch saltpeter
1 cup cold water

Grind meat and fat coarsely, add seasonings, and grind again with finer plate. Stir well, while adding water.

Separate casings into lengths of 1 to 1½ feet. Fill skins, tie at each end, and twist in the middle to make two long, thin sausages each.

Hang to dry in a cool place, 60 degrees at most. Leave for a whole day, then smoke for 8 hours. Smoking produces the deep, tawny brown frankfurter color. These sausages will keep for several weeks.

SAUCISSONS (LARGE SAUSAGES)

Saucisson Cuit au Madere
Sausage with Madeira

This large sausage is neither dried nor smoked; consequently, it will spoil rather quickly. Let it mature for 2 days, then eat it within 7 days. Like the other saucissons, this is sliced finely and served as an hors d'oeuvre.

1 lb. good, lean center-cut pork loin	2 tbsp. salt
½ lb. hard fat back	pinch of quatre-épices
2 oz. chopped truffles (optional)	pinch of white pepper
	2 tbsp. Madeira
	8 to 10 pistachio nuts, blanched

Grind meat and fat as finely as possible, two or three times. Season after the first time with salt and spices, then put through machine again. Finally, stir in Madeira, truffles, and pistachios.

Put into nice piece of large intestine, and tie each end. Wrap in a fine muslin and tie once again, like a parcel, not just at each end.

Simmer for 45 minutes, then hang to cool and dry. Tighten up the string and the cloth, and store in an airy place.

Saucisson de Ménage (or de Campagne)

This sausage is left to dry and mature instead of being eaten right away like a small sausage. It is sliced and served uncooked.

2 lbs. lean pork from neck or shoulder	4 heaping tbsp. salt
1 lb. hard fat back	1 tsp. black pepper
1 tsp. saltpeter	1 tsp. sugar
1 clove garlic, crushed	1 tsp. quatre-épices

Grind meat and fat once, and mix in seasonings and saltpeter, which will turn sausage a rosy pink. Fill some large intestines, tying to make one or two sausages. Keep in mind that they will shrink by about a third.

Hang in a well-aired place at a steady temperature of 60 degrees for 3 to 5 days, depending on the season. Keep away from steam or direct sunlight. Then hang on a hook in a cool, airy, place, and don't be tempted to try them before a month is up—better still, 2 to 3 months. When they start to shrink, squeeze them down from each end so that the insides will be well compacted and easy to slice.

Saucisson à l'Ail
Garlic Sausage

2 lbs. lean pork from neck or shoulder
½ lb. hard fat back
good pinch cayenne
small pinch saltpeter
1 clove garlic, crushed

½ tsp. quatre-épices
2 heaping tbsp. salt
½ tsp. black pepper
1 tsp. whole black peppercorns
2 tbsp. brandy

Grind lean meat well, and add seasonings except for peppercorns and brandy. Grind two more times. Chop pork fat into small dice, and add it together with peppercorns and brandy to ground meat. Mix together well with your hands for 10 minutes. Fill skins firmly, pressing mixture down well. Hang from a hook in an airy place (60 degrees) for 4 days; then string and store at about 50 degrees for 5 months.

Saucisson de Lyons

There is not a great deal of difference among the large sausages of Lyons, Arles, Lorraine, and Burgundy. Sometimes beef is added to the pork, or a glass of liqueur, sometimes the fat is cut in strips, sometimes ground, but otherwise the method is the same, and after a maturing period the various types are all eaten raw, in thin slices, with bread, as an hors d'oeuvre or a snack.

2 lbs. leg of pork, weighed without bone or fat	2 rounded tbsp. salt quatre-épices
½ lb. hard fat back or fat bacon	½ tsp. white peppercorns, ground
1 tbsp. sugar	pinch saltpeter

Finely grind and pound lean pork, add seasonings, and mix well. An electric mixer will take the hard work out of stirring the lean meat and spices. Cut fat into small strips, and mix with pork. See that the fat is well distributed, but take care that you don't reduce it to a hash like the lean pork. Stuff filling well down into large beef intestine, tying it into 18-inch lengths.

Hang from hook in a cool, airy place. The temperature should be a steady 60 degrees or a little under, with no dampness or direct sunlight, for the first few days. After 3 or 4 days, take sausages down, push filling tightly together from the two ends, and tie sausages up firmly so that the remain straight as they mature. Put four lines of string the length of the sausage, then wind the string round and round. Don't cut into lots of separate bands of string, because you will need to pull it up tighter during the long maturing time.

Now put saucissons away in a dry, well-aired larder, hanging from a hook so they there is good air circulation all around them, and forget they are there—apart from an occasional tightening of strings. Leave them for 6 months; if you try to eat them too soon, they will taste horrible.

Saucisson d'Arles

³/₄ lb. lean beef	6 tbsp. salt
2 lbs. leg of pork, weighed without bone or fat.	1 tsp. black pepper
	1 tsp. whole peppercorns
¹/₂ lb. fat back or bacon	1 tsp. quatre-épices
2 tbsp. sugar	

Follow the method for Saucisson de Lyons, grinding the lean meat finely and keeping the fat in short strips.

Saucisson de Lorraine

1 lb. shoulder of pork, weighed without bone or fat	¹/₂ tsp. ground white pepper
¹/₂ lb. lean beef	1 tsp. sugar
¹/₂ lb. fat from neck	2 heaping tbsp. salt
	¹/₂ tsp. quatre-épices

Follow the method for Saucisson de Lyons.

Saucisson de Bourgogne

1 lb. lean neck or shoulder of pork, weighed without bone	1 tsp. white pepper
	¹/₄ cup Kirsch
¹/₂ lb. hard fat back or bacon	2 heaping tbsp. salt
	¹/₂ tsp. quatre-épices

Grind lean and fat pork together, stir, and season well. Follow the method for Saucisson de Lyons.

Saucisson à Trancher
Slicing Sausage

2 lbs. sowbelly, equal parts lean and fat	2 heaping tbsp. salt
1 tsp. quatre-épices	1 tsp. black pepper
2 or 3 cloves garlic	4 tbsp. chopped parsley

Grind meat well, add seasonings, and fill large intestines, pushing meat well down. Simmer for 2 to 3 hours in salted water, drain, dry, and hang at a steady temperature of 60 degrees for at least a month.

SAUCISSONS FUMÉS (SMOKED SAUSAGES)

In the nineteenth century, sausages were hung up in the farmhouse chimney to smoke very gently until they were dry and white. Then they were restrung and dipped in wine lees in which had been boiled sage, bay leaves, and thyme. A day or two on the hook to dry, a month or two of maturing, wrapped in paper in a box of wood ashes, and they were ready to eat.

Saucisson de Ménage Fumé

Follow procedure for Saucisson de Ménage, adding an additional 2 teaspoons sugar, 1 teaspoon black pepper, and 2 cloves garlic.

Hang on a hook to dry, at a temperature of 60 degrees for 3 to 5 days, then smoke for a few days, until sausage is a beautiful deep, yellowish brown. Hang in a cool, airy larder for a month.

Saucisson de Provence

2	lb. lean pork from neck or shoulder	2	heaping tbsp. salt
³/₈	lb. hard fat back	1	tsp. black peppercorns
¹/₄	lb. lean sowbelly	1	tsp. black pepper
	pinch of saltpeter	1	tsp. quatre-épices
		2	tsp. sugar

Grind lean pork and sowbelly well. Cut fat in strips, add to other meats, and mix in remaining ingredients. Hang on a hook to dry at a temperature of 60 degrees for 3 to 5 days, then smoke gently for 8 hours.

Saucisson au Foie de Porc
Large Pork Liver Sausage

1¹/₂	lbs. lean pork neck or shoulder weighed without bone	1	tsp. quatre-épices
1	lb. pork liver	2	heaping tbsp. salt
1	lb. cooked tongue	3	oz. truffles, chopped
2	oz. pistachio nuts, blanched	¹/₂	lb. leaf lard
1	tsp. black pepper	¹/₄	cup onions, chopped
			saffron dissolved in a little white wine

Grind meat, liver, and fat very small. Cut tongue into small dice, add with other ingredients except for white wine and saffron, and stir well. Leave for a day in a covered dish. Fill large beef intestine, pushing meat mixture firmly down. Tie at each end. Simmer in nearly boiling water for 45 minutes. Hang up to dry in an airy place at a steady temperature of 60 degrees, and leave for 5 weeks. Color the saucisson with some saffron dissolved in a little white wine, then smoke for about 6 hours.

Saucisson d'Italie
Italian Sausage

1 lb. lean pork neck or shoulder, weighed without bone	1 rounded and 1 level tbsp. of salt
1 lb. lean veal	1 heaping tsp. black pepper
½ lb. hard fat back	2 tbsp. ginger
½ pint pig blood	2 tbsp. cinnamon
	2 tbsp. nutmeg
	2 cups dry white wine

Grind lean meats. Cut fat into small dice, and add along with blood to lean meats. Season. Stir in wine, and mix everything well. The traditional casing is a pig's bladder, but use large intestines as an alternative. Dry for 3 to 5 days, hanging from a hook in an airy place at a steady temperature of 60 degrees. Smoke for 4 days over a smoldering fire, preferably of juniper branches. Brush with olive oil and keep in dry, cold place, 40 to 45 degrees, still hanging up. Leave to mature for at least a month.

Note: You can omit the smoking process and allow the saucisson to dry on the hook for 2 months.

Saucisson de Lyons Fumé
Smoked Lyons Sausage

---

1 lb. lean pork, weighed without bone or fat	1 tsp. whole black peppercorns
½ lb. fillet steak	½ tsp. black pepper
½ lb. fat back or Canadian bacon fat	1 tbsp. salt
4 shallots, chopped	2 cloves garlic, crushed
	pinch of saltpeter

Grind pork and fillet steak together twice; get meats as fine as you can. Pounding with a pestle or beating with an electric mixer will reduce meats to an even mass. Cut bacon into small dice, and mix in evenly. Add remaining ingredients. Leave mixture in a cool place for 24 hours.

Fill skins and tie them. Make a brine by adding ½ pound bay of unadulterated rock salt, ½ pound sugar (1¼ cups), and 1 heaping tablespoon saltpeter to 2 quarts water. Bring to boil, then remove from heat. Allow to cool. Place sausages in large glass or stoneware pot, and cover with cooled brine. Put a board or top to keep sausages entirely immersed. Cover pot, and leave sausages in brine for 6 days. Then drain and dry, and smoke very lightly for 4 days. Hang to dry at a temperature of 60 degrees. Leave to mature for at least a month, stringing and restringing as they shrink.

SAUCISSONS-CERVELAS
(LARGE BOILING SAUSAGES, OR SAVELOYS)

As far as a mixture goes, there is not much difference between these sausages and the smaller saucisses or the big saucissons and fumés. But as for size and maturing, they are a halfway stage between the two. Choose skins that will give you a diameter of about 1½ inches, and as you fill them, twist every 8 to 12 inches, longer if you want to bend the sausages around and tie them together in a loop. You can smoke them lightly or not, as you please. You can salt them for 3 to 4 days in brine, or just hang them up in a cool place for 2 to 3 days.

Saucisson-Cervelas

½ lb. lean pork neck shoulder, weighed without bone	2 shallots, chopped
	½ clove garlic, crushed
	1 tbsp. salt
¼ lb. fillet steak	1 scant tsp. black pepper
¼ lb. fat bacon	small pinch of saltpeter

Grind lean meats, add seasonings, and grind again. Chop bacon into small dice, and mix in well. Fill skin, and tie at each end. Hang to dry at a temperature of 60 degrees for 2 days, or salt in brine for 2 to 3 days. Sausage also can be used straightaway, but it should be left for 24 hours for all the ingredients to blend well. It can be gently smoked for 6 hours.

To serve, prick with a sharp needle, and simmer in water or red wine for an hour. Makes 1 pound of sausage.

BOUDINS BLANCS (WHITE PUDDINGS)

In a contrast to the boudins noirs (black puddings), these succulent creamy white sausages are the most desirable in the charcuterie. The whitest pork is used, or chicken, or occasionally rabbit. Cream, eggs, onions, and ground rice or a few bread crumbs are added to make the mixture as bland and smooth textured as possible.

Using your sausage-making attachment, you can easily make these delicate boudins. Simmer in a ham or fish boiler with strainer, a metal salad shaker, or a french fry basket. Boudins need to be lowered into the water and lifted out with a minimum of fuss and handling, or they will burst.

Boudins Blancs de Paris

½ lb. roasted or uncooked chicken breast	3 eggs
½ lb. pork from loin	¾ lb. onions, chopped
1¼ lb. leaf lard or hard fat back	2 scant tbsp. salt
¾ cup bread crumbs, soaked in ¼ cup hot milk or cream	1 tsp. finely ground white pepper
	1 tsp. quatre-épices or other spices

Grind meats and fat as finely as possible, add seasonings, and put through grinder again with onions. Add bread crumbs with milk or cream, and eggs, and beat well. Fill skins, but not too tightly or they will burst while cooking. Tie (twisting is not enough) with heavy white thread into 6-inch sausages.

Place 5 cups water and 2½ cups milk in large pan. Bring to boil, and lower strainer basket of sausages into hot liquid. Keep temperature just below a boil, or sausages will burst. Prick with a needle as they rise to the surface. Simmer for 20 minutes, timed from when liquid returned to just below a boil. Raise strainer carefully, and leave it to drain completely over bowl. The next day, prick sausages, brush with melted butter, and fry.

Boudins Blancs du Mans

½ lb. lean pork from neck or leg	½ cup cream
1¼ lbs. fresh hard fat back	2 scant tbsp. salt
¾ cup chopped onion	1 tsp. fine white pepper
1 egg	4 heaping tbsp. chopped fresh parsley

Follow method for Boudins Blancs de Paris.

Boudins Blancs

½ lb. white chicken meat	10 egg whites
½ lb. pork loin or tenderloin	2 tbsp. salt
¾ lb. leaf lard	1 tsp. finely ground white pepper
2¼ cups milk	
2 rounded tbsp. ground rice	1 tsp. quatre-épices

Boil milk and pour into ground rice, stirring well to avoid lumps. Return to pan and cook gently until thick. Grind meat and fat two or three times. Whirl in blender with a little milk and rice mixture, or put through sieve. Add remaining ingredients and mix thoroughly. Finish according to the method of Boudins Blancs de Paris.

Boudins de Lapin (or de Lievre)

¼ lb. pork tenderloin	2 shallots, chopped fine
¼ lb. hard fat back	1 onion, chopped fine
1½ lbs. rabbit or hare, weighed without bones	butter
1 rabbit liver	4 heaping tbsp. chopped mixed parsley, chives, and tarragon
4 tbsp. blood	2 tbsp. salt
1½ cups fresh white bread crumbs	½ tsp. fine white pepper
½ cup milk	½ tsp. quatre-épices
2 eggs	

Note: You don't need skins for this boudins, though they can be made in conventional sausage style with success.

Make a thick paste of bread crumbs and milk by boiling milk in pan, then stirring in bread crumbs until mixture is fairly solid. Cook slowly until mixture, or panada, comes away from side of pan. Remove from heat, and leave to cool completely.

Grind lean and fat meat together well. If you have an electric blender, drop the pieces of meat into the blades and moisten with one or both eggs as necessary. Beat this smooth meat mixture with the cold panada. Sauté chopped onion and shallots in a little butter over low heat. When they are a golden mush, stir in blood and liver, and go on cooking gently.

Mix everything together, adding eggs if you didn't use them before. If you don't have a beater, squeeze and knead with your hands until everything is well mixed. Form mixture into little round balls, the usual meatball size, and drop them into simmering water for 10 minutes. Drain, cool, coat with egg and bread crumbs, and fry in butter.

Chorizos

This Spanish sausage is very popular in France, especially in the Southwest, where it is added to thick vegetable soups and cassoulets. The peppery seasonings can be varied to taste.

1 lb. lean pork from neck or shoulder	1/4 tsp. sugar
1/2 lb. hard fat back	2 tbsp. salt
1 whole red sweet pepper or small chili pepper	1/4 tsp. cayenne
1/4 cup red wine	1 large clove garlic, crushed
	good pinch of saltpeter

Cut red or chili pepper in half, remove seeds and stem carefully, and put through coarse plate of grinder with lean and fat pork. Add remaining ingredients, and fill wide (1-inch-diameter) sausage skins, twisting every 5 to 6 inches. Smoke lightly or dry above stove overnight at a temperature between 60 and 70 degrees.

Mortadelle

This sausage is a pale pink color, studded with small cubes of white fat and peppercorns.

1 lb. lean pork, weighed without bone	1 tsp. saltpeter
½ lb. hard fat back	2 heaping tbsp. salt
¾ lb. salted fat back or fat bacon	1 tsp. peppercorns
	1 tsp. coriander

Grind lean pork and fresh pork fat to a close, fine mass. Cut salted fat into small cubes, and mix everything together. Lay a fine cloth on strainer dish or grid, and let mixture drain overnight. Here again the casing traditionally is a pig's bladder, but a piece of large intestine may be used. Tie the two ends, and soak in Italian brine.

Italian Brine: Put 1½ quarts of water on to boil with 2 heaping tablespoons saltpeter, 2½ pounds sea salt (or unadulterated rock salt), and ⅛ cup bicarbonate of soda. Stir everything together well, and let boil for a moment or two. Add 1½ quarts dry white wine and 1 ounce mixed spices (peppercorns, cloves, and cinnamon), tied in a little cloth bag. Remove immediately from heat, and let brine cool down completely.

Take out bag of spices, and put sausage into brine. After 5 days (10 if you are using pig's bladder), remove sausage, drain well, and smoke for 4 days. Then cook in nearly boiling water for 3 hours (1½ hours for smaller mortadelle sausages in large intestines). Drain, dry with a cloth, and hang for 30 days to mature.

GERMANY

The best-known German sausage in the United States is the frank-furter, which originates from the city of Frankfurt.

Sausage was introduced during the Middle Ages to north-central Europe, now considered the "sausage center" of the world, and most north-central European sausages have their roots in Germany.

With the region's cooler climate and cool cellars, much experimentation could be done in the preserving of meat. Here, the *wurstmacher* often became more popular and respected than the mayor, and he became quite wealthy with his secret recipes.

Germany has over 1,456 kinds of sausage, and everyone has his favorite. The nation wolfs down an estimated one billion pounds of sausage a year. More sausage is consumed per person in Germany than any other place in the world. In Berlin and the north, a popular delicacy is blutwurst, or blood sausage, a dark red sausage dotted with white specks of fat. Popular belief has it that eating blood sausage before sundown is a sure way to make money and avoid catching a fever for a whole year.

Although all German cities are well known for their sausage, the real mecca is Munich. The Bavarian capital is a monument to the wurst. Munich's most colorful setting for sausage eating is the early morning outdoor food market, where wurst stands abound. Another exciting place to find people enjoying the popular wurst is at the annual Munich beer festival, or Oktoberfest.

Nothing can compare with the traditional varieties of German sausage, temptingly flavored with everything from tomatoes to truffles, from honey to rum.

Bratwurst with Veal
Fry Sausage

1 lb. boneless pork shoulder	½ tsp. grated nutmeg
½ lb. boneless veal	1 tsp. black pepper
1½ tsp. salt	½ tsp. mace
	½ cup water

Cut meat into 1-inch cubes, and grind twice through fine plate of meat grinder. Mix seasonings in water. Pour over meat, and mix well with hands. Stuff into hog casings, and twist into 4- to 5-inch links. Refrigerate. Use within 2 to 3 days.

Bratwurst with Beef

3 lbs. pork shoulder blade, boneless, cubed	2 tbsp. salt
½ lb. lean beef, cubed	1½ tsp. black pepper
¼ pork fat, cubed	1½ tsp. coriander
1 tbsp. grated ginger	½ tsp. dried mustard

Grind pork, beef, and fat using coarse blade. Mix in remaining ingredients. Stuff into six 30-inch-long, ¾-inch wide casings, tying off four 6-inch sausages for each 30-inch length. Makes 24 links.

German Bratwurst

1 lb. coarse-ground pork
1 lb. coarse-ground veal or beef
2 tsp. ground celery seed
2 tsp. ground caraway seed
2 tbsp. dry milk
1 egg
2 tsp. onion powder
salt
black pepper
small amount of grated
   lemon peel
1 tsp. dried parsley
3 tbsp. water

Combine all ingredients, and mix well. Let sit 1 hour, then mix again. Stuff into casings or fry as patties. Best in casings.

Liverwurst
German-Style Liver Sausage

10 lbs. pork liver, raw	1 oz. white pepper
3 lbs. pork head meat, fresh	¼ oz. ground ginger
3 lbs. salted pork fat	¼ oz. marjoram
4 lbs. pork snouts	pinch cinnamon
¾ lb. onion	pinch cloves
10 oz. salt	

Cook meats except for liver in separate nets, using a minimum of cooking water. Cook snouts for 2 hours, head meat 45 minutes, and fat 15 minutes. Slice onion and deep-fry in lard. Break down raw liver and cooked onion on fine plate and snouts and cheeks through coarse plate. Transfer liver to bowl chopper and add seasonings followed by pork meats and finally fat. Continue chopping until mixture is a fine paste. You may need to add small quantities of cooking water during chopping. Fill meat into hog bungs, not too tightly, and cook sausage at 165 degrees for 1 hour. Chill sausage in ice water. Dry, then smoke for 3 hours at 110 degrees. Pig's brains are sometimes used in this type of sausage, but as they decompose rapidly they must be handled perfectly fresh.

Leberwurst
Liver Sausage

---

2 lbs. skinless fresh pork belly or side pork	1½ tsp. salt
1½ lbs. fresh pork liver	½ tsp. pepper
½ lb. lean pork shoulder	1 tsp. marjoram
2 large onions, sliced	½ tsp. thyme

Cut meat and liver into small pieces. Combine with onion, salt, and pepper. Add enough cold water to just cover. Bring to a boil, reduce heat, and simmer for ½ hour. Drain, reserving stock. Add herbs to meat mixture, and mix well. Let cool. Grind meat through coarse plate of meat grinder. Add a bit of the stock to moisten slightly. Stuff into casings, and twist into 4- to 5-inch lengths. Refrigerate. Use within 2 to 3 days.

Wurstchen

---

2 lbs. lean pork	2 tsp. black pepper
1 lb. veal	2 tsp. cardamom
1 lb. bacon	¾ cup Rhine wine
4 tsp. salt	

Cut up all meat with knife, and mix together. Sprinkle on salt and dry spices. Coarse grind once. Add wine, and fine grind as you stuff casings. Cook for 3 minutes in salted water, and cool. Must be cooked before eating.

Rindfleischkochwurste

2 lbs. fresh pork fat	2½ tsp. black pepper
3 lbs. lean beef	1¼ tsp. coriander
5 tsp. salt	⁵⁄₁₆ tsp. saltpeter

Chop meat with knife, add seasonings, and grind once. Stuff casings, then let dry for 2 days in a cold place. This sausage may be smoked.

Augsburgerwurste

2 lbs. lean pork	¾ tsp. cloves
1 lb. bacon	¾ tsp. nutmeg
3 tsp. salt	³⁄₁₆ tsp. saltpeter
1½ tsp. black pepper	

Dice pork and bacon into small pieces, and mix together with seasonings. Stuff casings, and smoke at 100 degrees in smokehouse for 4 hours. Poach for 30 minutes and serve.

German Sausage Meat

2 pork kidneys or
  1 pork heart
5 oz. porkbelly
4 oz. barley groats
2 pints water

ground pimiento
salt
black pepper
thyme

If using kidneys, split lengthwise, remove cores, and wash thoroughly. Cover with boiling water, and leave to soak for about an hour. If using heart, cut in half and remove skin, veins, and arteries. Wash well. Put kidneys or heart into 2 pints of boiling, slightly salted water with meat. Simmer gently until done, about 1½ hours. If necessary, bring the stock up to 2 pints with water. Bring again to a boil, sprinkle in barley groats, and simmer gently over low heat until done, about 2 hours. Chop meat finely and mix with groats. Season to taste with salt, pepper, pimiento, and thyme.

Gehirnwurst

2½ lbs. coarse-ground pork
2½ lbs. pork brains
  2 tbsp. salt

1 tbsp. black pepper
2 tsp. mace
1 cup water

Cook pork brains in salted, acidulated water (water made sour with a bit of vinegar) until done. Combine all ingredients, mix well, and stuff into hog casings.

Konogswurst

2½ lbs. coarse-ground chicken meat
2½ lbs. partridge meat
¾ cup mushrooms, chopped

2 eggs
2 tbsp. salt
2 tsp. mace
1 cup Rhine wine

Combine all ingredients, and mix well. Stuff into sheep casings.

Schwabischewurst

---

5 lbs. fine-ground pork butt
2 tbsp. salt
3 tsp. black pepper
3 tsp. sugar

6 cloves garlic, pressed
2 tbsp. caraway seed
1 cup cold water

Combine all ingredients, mix well, and stuff into hog casings.

GREECE

The first record of sausage comes from Greece: Homer refers to sausage in his *Iliad* and *Odyssey*, written in about the ninth century B.C. In the fifth century B.C., Aristophanes, in his comedy *The Clouds*, said, "Let them make sausage of me and serve me up to the students." And in the oldest known cookbook, also from Greece, sausages are mentioned. Salami also appears in Greek writings and is supposed to have been developed in the ancient city of Salamis on the eastern coast of Cyprus. This is where the word *salami* originated.

Yet although Greece was the birthplace of sausage, and the country developed many varieties, sausage has not reached the prominence it has in the Germanic north-central European area.

Present Greek sausages make much use of lamb and pork; very little beef is used.

Greek Pork Sausage

5 lbs. medium-ground pork butt	1/4 tsp. cayenne
	1/4 tsp. chili powder
1 large onion, finely chopped	1/4 tsp. allspice
	1/4 tsp. thyme
6 cloves garlic, pressed	2 bay leaves
2 tsp. black pepper	1/2 cup parsley, chopped
2 tsp. oregano leaves	1 cup water

Combine all ingredients, and mix well. Stuff into hog casings. Bake or fry.

Loukanika #1
Greek Sausage

1	lb. chopped lamb	1	tsp. black pepper
1	lb. chopped pork	1	tsp. crushed garlic
	thin rind of 1 orange,	1	tsp. cinnamon
	finely chopped	1	tsp. allspice
10 to 20	whole black pepper-	½	cup wine
	corns, cracked		lemon juice

Mix all ingredients except lemon juice, and marinate for 1 week in refrigerator, stirring every day. Fry one small portion to check seasoning; if necessary, add salt. Using proper attachment on meat grinder for stuffing, stuff mixture into casings separated into 12-inch lengths. Prick casings with fork. String stuffed casings up to dry, either in cold cellar or outdoors in cold weather, in a protected area for 1 week. Cut in 1-inch pieces and broil. Sprinkle with lemon juice and serve warm. Makes 2 to 2½ dozen.

Loukanika #2

Here is another variation of the Greek Sausage.

4½ lbs. boneless pork butt	1½ tsp. coriander
1 tbsp. thyme	¾ tsp. cracked bay leaves
1 tbsp. marjoram	1½ tbsp. grated orange peel
4 to 6 cloves garlic, minced or pressed	2½ to 3½ tsp. salt
1½ tsp. allspice	¾ cup dry red wine

Cut pork butt into cubes, separating lean meat and fat. Measure or weigh; you should have equal parts, or 2¼ pounds each, fat and lean meat. Grind coarsely. Combine ground meat in a bowl with remaining ingredients. Using your hands or a heavy spoon, mix well. Cover and chill at least 2 hours or overnight. Shape into patties or links.

Greek Orange Sausage

3 lbs. fine-ground pork butt	1 tbsp. allspice
2 lbs. fine-ground beef	1 tbsp. black pepper
3 cloves garlic, pressed	1 tbsp. salt
1 large orange	1 cup white wine
1 tbsp. cinnamon	

Put orange peel, garlic, cinnamon, allspice, pepper, salt, and wine in blender, and blend until orange peel is finely chopped. Mix well into meat, and stuff into hog casings or make patties.

HUNGARY

What sets Hungarian sausages apart is the liberal use of paprika, the ubiquitous ground red pepper that varies from sweet to hot. These delicious sausages are made on farms and in villages during pig-killing time in autumn.

Debreceni
Hungarian Paprika Sausage

1¾ lbs. pork butt	⅛ tsp. ground ginger
¾ lb. beef chuck	⅛ tsp. allspice
½ lb. pork back fat	1 tsp. curing salts
3 tbsp. sweet Hungarian paprika	(optional)
1½ tbsp. chopped garlic	1 tbsp. kosher salt
½ tsp. coriander	1 tsp. sugar
½ tsp. coarsely ground black pepper	½ cup water

Mix seasonings and sugar together, and rub all over pork, beef, and pork fat. Cover and refrigerate for 2 hours or overnight. Grind everything together through a ¼-inch plate into large bowl. Add the water and any liquid remaining from spice marinade. Knead and squeeze until everything is well blended. Be sure to include the optional curing salts if you are going to air-dry or cold smoke. To air-dry, place in front of a fan overnight; then cold smoke for 8 to 12 hours. Otherwise, you can dry the sausages lightly by refrigerating them, unwrapped, overnight. You also can hot smoke the sausage. Makes 2½ to 3 pounds.

Hazi Kolbasz

5 lbs. medium-ground pork	1½ tbsp. paprika
4 cloves garlic	½ tsp. ground cloves
2 tbsp. salt	1 lemon rind, grated
2 tsp. black pepper	1 cup water

Combine all ingredients, and stuff into hog casings. Bake for 1 hour at 350 degrees.

Hungarian Hurka

4 lbs. pork butt	1 tbsp. black pepper
2 lbs. pork butt	⅛ tsp. marjoram
1 lb. pork jowl	¼ cup salt
1 lb. pork liver	5 lbs. cooked rice
1 large onion, fried in ¼ cup lard	

Boil the meats, and grind through coarse blade. Add 1 cup juice from boiled meat. Mix together with remaining ingredients, and stuff into hog casings. Drop into boiling water. Boil for 1 minute, remove, and bake when ready to serve.

Hungarian Kolbasz

12 lbs. coarse-ground pork
1/4 cup salt
2 tbsp. black pepper
3 tbsp. paprika

1 tsp. cayenne
6 large cloves garlic
1 cup water

Cook garlic in water, then mash. Add seasonings to meat, and mix in liquid and garlic. Stuff into hog casings.

Majas Hurka
Hot Liver Sausage

1 lb. pork butt
2 lbs. pork liver
2 lbs. pork lungs
2 tbsp. salt
2 1/2 cups beef broth
(bouillon)

2 large onions
1/2 lb. lard
1 tbsp. black pepper
1 tsp. marjoram
1 cup uncooked rice

Boil pork liver and lungs together with 1 tablespoon salt. Cook rice in beef broth, and fry onions until soft. Combine all ingredients except rice, and put through fine plate of grinder. Add rice, mix well, and stuff into hog casings. Boil for 10 minutes, and then fry or bake.

IRELAND

Ireland has always had a great tradition of sausage making, and many of the emigrant Irish now living in England place regular orders with pork butchers in Dublin for a weekly supply of their favorite brand. Among the most popular are Hafners sausages of Dublin and the Hick sausages of Dalkey and Dun Laoghaire. In Ireland, sausages are eaten for breakfast, lunch, tea, cocktails, and picnics.

Irish Sausage

5	lbs. coarse-ground pork butt	3	tsp. thyme
5	cups bread crumbs	3	tsp. basil
4	eggs, lightly beaten	3	tsp. rosemary
8	cloves garlic, pressed	3	tsp. marjoram
1	tbsp. salt	3	tsp. black pepper
		2	cups water

Combine all ingredients, mix well, and stuff into sheep casings. Fry in butter or oil.

ISRAEL

Israeli Salami #1

5 lbs. medium-ground beef chuck	1 cup white wine
4 tbsp. salt	1 tbsp. paprika
3 tbsp. sugar	2 tsp. ground ginger
1 tbsp. black pepper	1 tsp. nutmeg
	8 cloves garlic, pressed

Combine all ingredients, and mix well. Refrigerate for 48 hours, then stuff into fiber or cellulose casings. Cool smoke for 6 to 8 hours. Slowly increase the temperature to 150 to 160 degrees, or until the internal temperature is 150 degrees. Chill the sausage in cold water, and dry for 5 to 8 weeks.

Israeli Salami #2

5 lbs. medium-ground beef	$\frac{1}{2}$ tsp. cardamon
1 tbsp. white pepper	8 cloves garlic, pressed
1 tsp. coriander	1 tbsp. sugar
$\frac{1}{2}$ tsp. nutmeg	4 tbsp. salt
1 cup white wine	

Follow instructions for Israeli Salami #1.

Israeli Salami #3

5	lbs. fine-ground beef chuck	3	tsp. coriander
4	tbsp. salt	1	tbsp. sugar
10	cloves garlic, pressed	1	cup white wine
1½	tsp. white pepper		

Follow instructions for Israeli Salami #1.

ITALY

Sausage has been an important part of Italian food culture for many hundreds of years. The early Romans enjoyed this delicacy and cured meats for sausage by salting them down in vessels that had been used for oil or vinegar, covering them with wine, then straw and snow. One of the oldest volumes on cookery, the *Epicius*, lists a number of sausage recipes often served in the homes of Roman patricians. The demands for pork must have been fairly heavy; in the second century A.D. Emperor Severus issued an edict to prevent the slaughter of sows and suckling pigs.

The Romans' liking for sausage was so great that no festive occasion was considered complete without it. Two of these celebrations were the Lupercalia and the Floralia, pagan orgies of feasting, drinking, and wenching. The association of sausage with these occasions caused the early church to look upon sausage as heathen and licentious. The revelry so upset the pious Constantine the Great, the first Christian emperor, that he banned both holidays and the making of sausage.

But no emperor's edict could stop a sausage lover, and Roman sausage bootleggers sold their wares despite the ban. Like the American experiment with prohibition centuries later, it became clear as time went by that the outlawed item could not be stamped out that way. Indeed, the prohibition was worse than sanction, so the church repealed its ban on sausage. Sausage has had a rightful place on Christian tables ever since.

The warm climate of Italy encouraged the development of the dry sausage. It had to be preserved with an abundance of salt and spices, then dried, generally without smoking. Many a delectable sausage today was named for an Italian city—Milano, Genoa, Bologna, and so forth.

Italian Sausage #1

8 lbs. pork shoulder
4 tbsp. salt
3 tbsp. fennel seed
2 tsp. black pepper
2 tsp. ground red pepper (optional)

Grind pork through coarse grinder plate. Add salt, fennel seed, black pepper, and red pepper (if hot sausage is desired), and mix with your hands. Fill casings. Let stand for a day or so before using. This sausage may be smoked or frozen, if desired. For a less greasy sausage, puncture each link in a couple of places when cooking.

Italian Sausage #2

2 lbs. pork butt
1/2 tsp. dried red pepper
1/2 tsp. salt
1 clove garlic

1 tsp. fennel seed
1/2 tsp. black pepper
2 oz. water or red wine

Coarse-grind meat or dice into 1/4-inch cubes. Mince garlic, and soak in wine or water. Blend all meat and liquid. Fill casings using funnel and spoon. Serves 8 to 10.

Italian Sausage #3

5 lbs. coarse-ground pork butt
1 tbsp. salt
1 tbsp coarse black pepper
5 cloves garlic, pressed
1 tbsp. fennel seed
1 tsp. anise seed
1 cup cold water
1 tbsp crushed hot pepper (optional)

Combine all ingredients, and mix well. Stuff into hog casings or make patties.

	Italian Sausage 5 Varieties of Flavor				
Ingredients	1	2	3	4	5
ground pork	6 lbs.	5 lbs.	5 lbs.	5 lbs.	5 lbs.
cure mix	—	1½ cups	1½ cups	—	—
liquid smoke		2½ tsp.	—	—	—
salt	⅛ cup	—	—	3 tbsp.	⅛ cup
water	—	2 cups	2 cups	½ cup	—
white pepper	—	1 tsp.	—	—	—
black pepper	—	5 tsp.	—	—	1½ tsp.
cayenne pepper	4 tsp.	—	¼ tsp.	—	—
chili pepper	—	—	—	—	1½ tsp.
whole peppercorns	—	1¼ tsp.	1 tsp.	1 tsp.	—
coriander	⅛ tsp.	—	—	—	—
garlic powder	—	¼ tsp.	—	—	½ tsp.
ground cloves	½ tsp.	—	—	—	—
onion powder	½ tsp.	—	—	—	—
paprika	½ tsp.	—	—	—	—
fennel	2 tsp.	¼ tsp.	1½ tsp.	—	1½ tsp.
rosemary	¼ tsp.	—	—	—	—
thyme	¼ tsp.	—	—	—	—
anise	—	¼ tsp.	—	—	—

Sweet Italian Sausage

5 lbs. coarse-ground pork butt	1 cup white wine
3 tsp. fennel seed	1½ tsp. sage leaves
2 tsp. white pepper	5 cloves garlic, pressed
	3 tsp. salt

Combine all ingredients, and mix well. Stuff into hog casings or make patties.

Fresh Italian Sausage: Sweet

10 lbs. boneless pork butt	3 tsp. fennel seed
6 tbsp. salt	2 tsp. coarse black pepper
1 pint ice water	1 tbsp. sugar

Chill meat between 30 and 34 degrees before starting. Remove and throw out all blood clots, cord, bones, and so on. Grind pork butts through ¼-inch or ³⁄₁₆-inch plate, and place into mixer. Add remaining ingredients, and mix well until evenly blended. Stuff into 32- to 35-millimeter hog casings. Hang on smoke sticks, and place in cooler. Sausage may be smoked. Do not keep sausage at room temperature any longer than necessary.

Italian Sausage: Mild

---

   1 lb. ground pork
   1 tsp. salt
  1/4 tsp. black pepper
   1 tsp. fennel seed
  1/4 tsp. crushed red peppers

Combine all ingredients, and mix well. For 1 or 2 pounds of sausage, store in refrigerator until ready to use. Then form into patties, and fry over low heat.

For larger batches, stuff into hog casings and twist into 4-inch links. If sausage is to be used within a few days, store in refrigerator; if it will be kept for a month or so, freeze.

Italian Sausage: Hot

---

   1 lb. ground pork
   1 tsp. salt
  1/4 tsp. black pepper
   1 tsp. crushed red peppers
   1 tsp. fennel seed

Follow procedure for Italian Sausage: Mild.

Fresh Italian Sausage: Mildly Hot

10 lbs. boneless pork butt	1 tbsp. sugar
6 tbsp. salt	3 tsp. crushed hot peppers
1 pint ice water	1 tsp. caraway seeds
1 tbsp. cracked fennel seed	1 tbsp. coriander

Follow instructions for Fresh Italian Sausage: Sweet.

Dry Italian Sausage

5 lbs. pork butt	2 tsp. black pepper
1 clove garlic, chopped	3 tsp. salt
1 wine glass red wine	3 tsp. fennel seed
1 tsp. cayenne pepper	1¾ tsp. Modern Cure

Place all ingredients in large bowl or pan, and mix thoroughly by hand until well blended. Store in refrigerator overnight. Stuff casings firmly, tying each securely. Hang in cool, dry, ventilated place for 1 week, then freeze.

Italian Pepper Sausage

4½ lbs. coarse-ground pork	1 cup red wine
1½ lbs. salt pork	4 tsp. fennel
2 tbsp. crushed red pepper, dried	1 clove minced garlic
¼ tsp. thyme	1 small onion, chopped finely
1½ tbsp. freshly ground black pepper	¼ tsp. coriander
	2 tbsp. salt
½ tsp. bay leaf, crushed	4 tbsp. paprika

Combine all ingredients, and mix well. Stuff into hog casings. Broil or fry.

Italian Cheese Sausage

7 lbs. boneless pork shoulder	4 tsp. fennel seeds, crushed
2 tsp. red pepper flakes, crushed	3 cloves garlic, minced fine
2 tsp. black pepper	1½ cups grated Parmesan
½ cup fresh parsley, finely chopped	1 cup dry red wine

Grind pork twice through coarse plate of meat grinder. Add remaining ingredients, and use hands to blend spices and cheese well. Stuff into hog casings, and twist into 4- to 5-inch links. Refrigerate. Use within 2 to 3 days, or freeze.

Italian Sweet Fennel Sausage

This mildly flavored sausage is perfumed with the scents of fennel, allspice, and oregano.

3 lbs. pork butt	1 tbsp. black pepper
¾ lb. pork back fat	⅛ tsp. ground allspice
4 garlic cloves, minced	1 tsp. dried oregano
4 tsp. kosher salt	½ cup dry red wine
2 tbsp. fennel seed	

Grind pork and fat together through ⅜-inch plate. Add garlic, salt, spices, and red wine. Mix well with your hands. Shape into patties, or stuff into medium hog casings and tie into 5-inch links. Makes 4 pounds.

Italian Brand Sausage

50 lbs. pork (80% lean)	10 cups water
50 lbs. regular pork	1 lb. paprika
3½ lbs. nonfat dry milk	4 oz. black pepper
2 lbs. salt	2 oz. oregano
5 oz. monosodium glutamate	2 oz. fennel
2 oz. anise	

Grind pork through medium plate. Add all other ingredients, and mix for 5 minutes. Stuff in hog casings (use 4-inch links). Use fresh or frozen.

Italian Pork Sausage: Hot

100	lbs. pork trimmings	4	oz. mild red pepper,
1 lb., 8	oz. salt		crushed
4	oz. white pepper	2	oz. coriander
4	oz. fennel	2	oz. paprika

Chill trimmings, and grind through 1/4-inch or 3/8-inch plate. Sift seasonings into pork, mixing with a large fork. Stuff into hog casings or size 30 to 36 cellulose or collagen casings. Link or roll into rope-tie sausages.

Italian Pork Sausage: Sweet

100	lbs. pork trimmings
1	lb., 8 oz. salt
4	oz. white pepper
4	oz. fennel
2	oz. paprika

Follow procedure for Italian Pork Sausage: Hot.

Tuscan Sausage

Tuscany is famous for its wines and olive oils, and also for its delicately flavored sausages. What comes through here is not the heat and spice of the South, but rather the subtle aromas of herbs, tomatoes, and wine. The best match for these complex and richly flavored sausages is medium-bodied Chianti Classico from Tuscany.

3	lbs. pork butt	4	anchovy fillets, finely
1/2	lb. pork back fat		chopped
2	tsp. kosher salt	1/4	cup basil, minced
1/2	cup chopped sun-dried	2	tbsp. chopped oregano
	tomatoes, packed in		pinch allspice
	olive oil	1/2	cup Chianti or other
2	tsp. coarsely ground		dry red wine
	black pepper		

Grind pork meat through 3/8-inch plate, and fat through 1/4-inch plate. In large bowl, knead meat, fat, and remaining ingredients. Mix until well blended. Stuff into medium hog casings, and tie into 6-inch links. Will keep 3 days in refrigerator. Makes 4 pounds.

Barese-Style Sausage

This popular sausage made in the style of Bari in southern Italy contains cheese. Don't store this sausage too long in the refrigerator or freezer, as the cheese can become quite strong with age and overpower the other flavors.

2	lbs. lean pork butt	1	tbsp. chopped garlic
1	lb. beef chuck	1	tbsp. kosher salt
1	lb. pork back fat	1	tbsp. red pepper flakes
1	cup cubed Pecorino or Romano cheese	1/4	cup fresh Italian parsley, chopped
1	tbsp. black pepper	1/2	cup dry red wine
1	tbsp. ground fennel seed		

In large bowl, toss together meat, fat, and cheese. Grind through 3/8-inch plate. Add remaining ingredients, and knead well. Stuff into medium hog casings, and tie into 4-inch links. Keeps for 2 to 3 days in the refrigerator or 1 to 2 months frozen. Makes 4 1/2 pounds.

Cotechino

5	lbs. coarse-ground fresh ham with skin	1	cup cold water
2	tbsp. salt	2	tsp. cinnamon
1 1/3	tbsp. coarse black pepper	2	tsp. cayenne
2	tbsp. nutmeg	1/2	cup Parmesan cheese
		1	tsp. ground cloves

Combine all ingredients, and mix well. Stuff into hog casings. Refrigerate for 2 days before eating or freezing.

Capicola

5	lbs. pork butt	4	tbsp. paprika
4	tbsp. salt	2	tbsp. ground red pepper
1	tbsp. sugar	1	cup red wine

Dice pork butt into 1-inch cubes. Combine all ingredients, and mix well. Refrigerate for 48 hours. Stuff into beef casings, and dry for 12 to 16 weeks. Lightly smoke if desired.

Milano Salami

15	lbs. fresh lean beef	2	oz. ground white pepper
25	lbs. lean pork	$\frac{1}{2}$	oz. fresh garlic
10	lbs. fat pork	22	oz. salt
4	oz. sugar	$1\frac{1}{2}$	oz. sodium nitrate
2	oz. whole white peppercorns		

Break beef down through $\frac{3}{8}$-inch plate with garlic, and then through $\frac{1}{8}$-inch plate. Put pork through $\frac{3}{8}$-inch plate. Mix all ingredients in mixer for about 2 minutes. Pack down in 6-inch layers. Store at 40 degrees until mixture has assumed a bright color. Stuff rightly into hog bungs, taking great care to avoid airlocks. Hang to dry for 36 hours, and wrap with hemp twine, about $\frac{1}{2}$ inch apart. Hang with good air circulation at a temperature of 45 to 55 degrees, and hold for 9 to 10 weeks.

Genoa Salami

50 lbs. lean pork trimmings, cured	1 lb. salami seasoning flour
15 lbs. pork back fat, cured	½ lb. sugar
35 lbs. lean beef chuck, without sinews, cured	2 oz. garlic compound

Dice fat in ¼-inch pieces, and run beef and pork through ¼-inch plate. Combine all ingredients, using enough flour to reach the desired consistency, and mix well. Spread 6 to 8 inches thick on boards, and place in cooler for 48 hours at 38 to 40 degrees. Stuff into hog bungs cut about 20 inches long. Hang in dry cooler for 36 to 48 hours after stuffing, then hang in a dry room at 48 to 56 degrees. This sausage is not smoked and should hang until firm and dry on surface. Then wrap with flax twine, starting at small end. Make loops 2 inches apart, and use slip hitch knots.

Catania Salami

5 lbs. medium-ground pork butt	½ tbsp. white pepper
4 tbsp. salt	¼ tsp. nutmeg
2 tbsp. sugar	½ tsp. ground coriander
1 tbsp. black pepper	1 tsp. fennel
	1 cup sweet vermouth

Combine all ingredients, and mix well. Refrigerate for 48 hours. Stuff into beef or fiber casings, and tie off into 10-inch links. Dry for 10 to 12 weeks.

Soppresatta Salami

2 lbs. coarse-ground beef chuck	1 tbsp. black pepper
3 lbs. medium-ground pork butt	2 tsp. white pepper
4 tbsp. salt	$\frac{1}{2}$ tsp. ground coriander
	10 cloves garlic, pressed
	1 cup red wine

Combine all ingredients, and mix well. Refrigerate for 48 hours. Stuff into large hog or beef casings, and tie off into 4-inch links. Dry for 8 to 12 weeks.

LITHUANIA

Sausage making in Lithuania is closely allied with that in the other countries bordering the North Sea.

Desros

10 lbs. fresh pork shoulder
2 lbs. onion, chopped
1 tbsp. allspice
1 tbsp. pepper
⅓ cup salt

Cook onions in small amount of fat until transparent. Cut meat in very small pieces or grind coarsely. Add onions with fat in which they were cooked, pepper, allspice, and salt. Combine thoroughly. Stuff into washed hog casings, and boil for about 1 hour. To reheat, brown in frying pan or oven.

Note: Instead of frying in fat, onions may be simmered in 2 cups of water. Onions with liquid then are added to chopped meat.

Lithuanian Sausage

9 lbs. boneless fresh pork shoulder	¼ cup butter
1½ lbs. smoked pork butt	3 tbsp. black pepper
1 cup chopped onion	2 tsp. white pepper
2 cloves garlic, minced	2 tsp. allspice

Grind meats once through coarse plate of meat grinder. Sauté onion and garlic in butter until limp, about 5 minutes. Cool and add to meat, along with seasonings. Stuff into hog casings, and twist or tie into 4- to 5-inch lengths. Add ¼ cup salt to 2 quarts water, and soak the links. Place in refrigerator overnight. Drain and pat dry with paper towels. Store in refrigerator. Use within 2 or 3 days or freeze.

MARTINIQUE

Martinique Pork Sausage Cakes

2 lbs. boneless fat pork	¼ tsp. cayenne
¾ tsp. thyme	1½ tsp. salt
1 tsp. sage	½ tsp. black pepper
⅛ tsp. allspice	

When buying pork, be sure it has not been trimmed of fat. Grind meat twice. Mix ground pork with seasonings, and let stand in refrigerator several hours or overnight before using. Shape mixture into 2-inch flat cakes, and fry until browned and cooked through. Any unused portion may be shaped into cakes and frozen for future use. Makes about 18 sausage cakes.

MEXICO

There is no sausage specifically of Mexican origin. The most prevalent sausage in Mexico is the Spanish chorizo.

Chorizo al Hogar
Homemade Mexican Sausages

---

1 lb. ground pork
1 tbsp. coarse-ground
    red chili pepper
    pinch of ground cloves

1 tsp. coriander
    pinch of cumin
1 tsp. oregano

Mix all ingredients together thoroughly, and make into four patties. Use in stuffing as is, or dry out in skillet over low heat, until fat stops running.

Salchicha Mexicana
Mexican Sausage

---

3 lbs. pork	2 cloves garlic
12 chilies anchos, peeled, seeded	2 tbsp. salt
	1 tbsp. black pepper
1 cup vinegar	½ tsp. cumin

Cut meat into tiny pieces, and place in deep bowl. Soak chilies in enough water to cover for 10 minutes. Drain and grind with pepper, cumin, salt, and garlic. Mix with diced meat. Add vinegar, and mix well with hands. Allow mixture to stand 24 hours in a cool place or in refrigerator.

Cut and wash 5 yards of sausage casings very well in water and then in vinegar. Stuff with prepared mixture, making each sausage about 4 inches long by tying each with dried corn leaves cut in strips or with cord. Make several pinpricks in each sausage to allow air to escape. Dry in sun for at least 4 days.

Mexican Chorizo Sausage

4½ lbs. boneless pork butt	5 to 8 cloves garlic, minced or pressed
10 to 12 dried New Mexico chilies (about 4 oz.)	2½ to 3½ tsp. salt
1 cup red wine vinegar	1½ tbsp. oregano
1 medium onion, quartered	1 tsp. cumin
	¼ to ¾ tsp. cayenne

Soak chilies in vinegar until soft, 3 hours to overnight. Remove stems. Place chilies and vinegar into blender with quartered onion, and puree. Cut pork butt into cubes, separating lean meat and fat. Measure or weigh; you should have equal parts, or 2¼ pounds each, lean meat and fat. Coarsely grind meat and fat. In large bowl, combine meat with all other ingredients. Mix with hands or a heavy spoon. Cover; chill at least 2 hours or overnight. Shape into patties or links.

THE NETHERLANDS

Liver Sausage

In rural areas, this sausage is often called "puddin' meat."

25 lbs. pork trimmings	black pepper
10 lbs. beef or veal	chopped onions
8 to 10 lbs. pork liver	(optional)
4 loaves stale bread or	mace, celery seed,
4 lbs. whole wheat flour	cardamom, and
salt	coriander (optional)

If beef or veal is not available, substitute pork. The use of pork liver, hearts, tongues, brains, sweetbreads, and kidneys along with some pork shoulder meat, combined with bread or whole wheat flour as a binder, makes a product that is very rich in vitamins and minerals.

Cook meats thoroughly, and reserve broth. Grind meats through fine blades along with bread. To this mixture, add 4 quarts of reserved broth, and season with salt and pepper. Chopped onions may be added if desired; mace, celery seed, cardamom, and coriander may be used to add flavor. After seasoning, cool mixture another 10 minutes, and pour into pans or crocks to harden. Then stuff into hog casings, cook a second time, dip into cold water to bleach, and hang in a cool place to dry. Alternatively, sausages may be placed in crocks without bleaching, and covered with hot lard to preserve for future use.

NORWAY

Fleskepolse
Pork Sausage

1 lb. veal	1/2 tsp. nutmeg
1/2 lb. fresh pork	1 tsp black pepper
1 tbsp. salt	2 to 3 slices onion

Cut veal in small pieces, sprinkle with salt, and grind until fine in meat grinder. Cut pork in pieces, grind twice, then once with veal. Work spices and minced onion well into mixture, and fill into clean intestines. Boil sausages in plenty of water, slightly salted for 1/2 hours, carefully turning them around occasionally, so that the fat will form the outer layer of the sausages, and the meat will form the core. Do not under any circumstances prick sausages. When done, let drain on clean cloth. Keep in refrigerator.

Sorlands-Kumper
Raw Potato Sausages

1 lb. fresh pork or suet, cut fine	1 cup flour
12 raw potatoes	½ cup sugar
1 cup oatmeal	½ cup white pepper
1 tbsp. salt	½ tsp. ginger
1 tsp. thyme	½ pkg. seedless raisins

Mix well, and fill in sausage-shaped muslin bags, which have first been dipped in cold water. Drop sausages in boiling, salted water, and boil slowly for 1½ hours.

Korv
Potato Sausage

5 lbs. shoulder pork	3 cups chicken broth
2½ lbs. potatoes	1 tsp. salt
1 onion (size of an egg)	bay leaves
1½ tsp. salt	allspice
1 tsp. white pepper	

Finely grind meat, potatoes, and onions, and mix together. Add salt and pepper, and knead thoroughly. Gradually add chicken broth while kneading. Stuff into pork casings that have been soaked overnight in cold water. Sprinkle with salt, and let stand in refrigerator overnight. Then drop into boiling water, add 1 teaspoon salt, bay leaves, and allspice, and boil slowly for 1 hour.

Norwegian Sausage

3 lbs. coarse-ground
beef chuck
2 lbs. coarse-ground
pork butt
1½ tbsp. salt

1 cup cold water
4 medium onions, grated
1 tbsp. black pepper
2½ tsp. nutmeg

Combine everything, and mix well. Stuff into hog casings. Bake or fry.

THE PHILIPPINES

In the Philippines, with its tropical climate, where vegetables, fruits, and many small mammals were available year-round, there was not the necessity to preserve foods as in countries in the temperate zones. Pigs were a staple meat of the Philippines, but they were cooked whole and eaten before spoilage. Sausage was not introduced until the coming of the Spaniards in the sixteenth century.

Logonzio Sausage

This is a popular Filipino sausage.

11 lbs. pork	10 cloves garlic, chopped
10 to 20 tbsp. salt	20 tsp. paprika
10 tsp. black pepper	1¼ tsp. saltpeter
5 cups vinegar or apple cider	

Cut pork into small pieces or grind through a ⅜-inch plate. Add remaining ingredients, and mix well. Let stand 1 to 2 hours. Fill into pork casings, tie into links, and dry in sun or hang in smoker without smoke.

POLAND

Although kielbasa is the Polish word for sausage, kielbasa also can be found in the sausage heritage of Austria, Germany, and Italy, under a variety of spellings, such as kolbassy and kobasa. This old-fashioned sausage is generously seasoned and placed in natural casing. It's a delicious homemade sausage with snap and bite.

The size of Polish sausage distinguishes it from most other sausages. One sausage weighs about ½ pound and measures about 10 inches long by 1¼ inches in diameter. It is not quite as highly spiced as some sausages but is heavy with garlic.

Kielbasa #1
Fresh Polish Sausage

10 lbs. pork butt	6 tbsp. salt
1 tbsp. salt	2 cloves garlic
1 tbsp. coarse black pepper	1 heaping tsp. marjoram
1 pint ice water	

Chill meat between 30 and 34 degrees before starting. Remove and throw out all blood clots, bones, cords, and so on. Grind pork through ¼- to ³/₁₆-inch plate, and place in mixer. Add remaining ingredients, and mix well, until seasonings are evenly distributed. Use stuffer to fill 40- to 42-millimeter hog casings. Hang on properly spaced smoke sticks, and dry in cooler. Do not keep sausage at room temperature any longer than necessary.

Kielbasa #2

1½ lbs. pork butt
½ lb. boneless beef chuck
½ cup coarse salt
½ tsp. black pepper

1 large clove garlic
½ cup water
¼ tsp. nutmeg
½ tsp. salt

Cut meats into small pieces (1 by 2 inches). Mix with coarse salt in large bowl, add water to cover, and allow to cure for 12 hours. Cut or grind into ¼-inch pieces. Juice or mince garlic into ½ cup water, and allow to stand. Mix together all ingredients. Fill into casings about 6 to 7 inches long. Smoke for 2 to 3 hours over cool fire using hickory chips. Makes 8 to 10 servings.

Kielbasa #3

26 lbs. pork, some fat
   (part beef or wild
   game may be used)
10 tbsp. salt
3½ tbsp. black pepper
2 tbsp. marjoram

4 tbsp. garlic powder
½ cup dry cure
⅓ cup sugar
   sage, rosemary, thyme,
   and paprika (optional)

Mix seasonings with cubed meat, then put through coarse grinder or chop. Put in shallow pan and cure under refrigeration for 3 to 4 days. Stuff into pork casings, and tie in desired lengths. Do not stuff too firmly, as the casings shrink when cooked. Allow sausages to sit for a day or so, then prick with a needle in several places to let air escape. Cool smoke until colored, then increase smoker temperature to 175 degrees for 45 minutes to cook thoroughly. Alternatively, you may cool smoke only, and cook links before eating.

Smoked Kielbasa
Smoked Polish Sausage

10 lbs. pork butt	1 heaping tsp. marjoram
2 cups soy protein or nonfat dry milk	1 quart water
1 tbsp. sugar	6 tbsp. salt
1 tbsp. black pepper	1/2 tsp. cure
	2 cloves garlic

Trim off excess fat, and remove and throw out all blood clots, bone, sinews, cords, and so on. Grind all lean meat through 1/4-inch plate and all fat through 1/8-inch plate. Place in mixer along with other ingredients, and mix until evenly blended. Stuff into 40- to 42-millimeter hog casings. Hang on properly spaced smoke sticks, and let dry.

When stuffing sausage, it normally is hung on sausage sticks in the room where you are working. By the time you are finished stuffing, much of the sausage is already dry. You may then place sausages in smokehouse preheated to 130 degrees, with dampers wide open, for about 1 hour or until casings are dry and starting to take on a brown color, or you may place sausages in cooler and leave until casings are dry.

Polish Blood Sausage

2½ lbs. coarse-ground pork butt	1 tsp. ginger
2 qts. pig blood to which 2 tsp. vinegar have been added	2 tsp. baking powder
	1 tbsp. salt
2½ cups cooked rice or barley	1½ tsp. black pepper
	1½ tsp. allspice
	3 cloves garlic, pressed

Combine all ingredients, and mix well. Stuff into hog casings. *Note:* Vinegar keeps blood from coagulating.

Kiszka

3 lbs. coarse-ground cooked pork butt	1 tbsp. black pepper
2 lbs. cooked buckwheat	½ tsp. marjoram
	1 tbsp. salt

Combine all ingredients, and mix well. Stuff into hog casings.

PORTUGAL

Sausages are central to Portuguese eating and cooking. Every region has its own specialties, and every sausage maker his own secret.

The most popular Portuguese sausage is probably linguica, and is what is generally known in the United States as "Portuguese sausage."

Linguica
Portuguese Sausage

4	lbs. boneless pork butt	1	tbsp. paprika
2½ to 3½	tsp. salt	½	tsp. cinnamon
4 to 7	cloves garlic, minced or pressed	½	tsp. ground cloves
4 to 6	small dried hot chili peppers, crushed	½	tsp. allspice
		¼	cup cider vinegar
1	tbsp. coriander	½	cup cold water

Cut pork into cubes, separating lean meat and fat. Measure or weigh; you should have equal parts, or 2 pounds each, fat and lean meat. Grind coarsely. Combine ground meat in large bowl with remaining ingredients, and mix well with your hands or a heavy spoon. Cover and chill at least 2 hours or overnight. Shape into patties or links.

Chorizo

Ingredients	Chorizo 3 varieties of flavor		
	1	*2*	*3*
ground pork	5 lbs.	4 lbs.	5 lbs.
vinegar	—	½ cup	½ cup
cure mix	1½ cups	—	—
salt	—	4 tsp.	2 tbsp.
water	2 cups	—	1 cup
black pepper	—	2 tsp.	1 tsp.
red pepper (cayenne)	¼ tsp.	1 tsp.	1 tbsp.
garlic powder	½ tsp.	1 tsp.	1 tbsp.
paprika	1 tsp.	—	7 tsp.
cumin	—	½ tsp.	—
oregano	—	2 tsp.	1 tbsp.

Grind meat and peppers with coarse blade. Add remaining ingredients. Stuff into 12-inch-long, 1⅜-inch-wide casings, tying off 10-inch lengths.

Portuguese Chourico

Chourico is similar to linguica, but a different spice mixture and a bit of cayenne make it a hotter sausage.

3 lbs. pork butt	3 tbsp. red wine vinegar
½ lb. pork back fat	1 tsp. black pepper
4 tsp. kosher salt	½ tsp. marjoram
3 tbsp. Hungarian or Spanish paprika	1 tsp. cumin
1 tsp. cayenne	½ tsp. coriander
1 tbsp. minced garlic	1 tsp. curing salts (if cold smoking)

Cut all external fat off pork, and refrigerate this fat along with back fat. Cut lean meat into strips, and liberally coat with all remaining ingredients. If you are going to dry and cold smoke sausages, add curing salts; if you will hot smoke, leave them out. Pack meat into plastic tub or stainless steel bowl, cover, and refrigerate overnight. The next day, grind lean pork through very coarse (³/₈- or ½-inch) plate, and grind fat through ¼-inch plate. In large bowl, mix lean meat and fat along with any liquid and spices still remaining from marinade. Knead and squeeze mixture until all ingredients are thoroughly blended. Stuff into wide hog casings, and tie into 10-inch links.

ROMANIA

Haussalami
Salami

---

10 lbs. pork	2 to 4 cloves garlic
5 lbs. juicy beef	½ cup water
4 lbs. bacon	2 oz. white pepper

Put pork and beef through grinder several times. Leave to drain in a napkin for 24 hours. Boil garlic in water for 20 minutes. Discard garlic; reserve cooking water. Cube bacon fine, and mix well with meat, salt, pepper, and reserved water. Fill into casings, tying off pieces 4 inches long. Prick each section with a needle so that air can escape. Smoke for 3 weeks, then store in cool place, about 48 degrees.

Bratwurst Sausages

---

6 lbs. pork shoulder
   salt
   black pepper
   grated garlic
2 cups water

Use only juicy meat. Chop pork fine, mix with salt, pepper, and garlic, and knead with water until smooth. Use funnel or sausage filler to fill into twenty 8-inch-long, 1-inch-diameter sausage casings. Prick each casing with a needle so that air can escape. Place sausages in cold water, and smoke after 2 days.

Carnati de Carne de Porc si Vaca
Pork and Beef Sausage

2	lbs. pork meat with fat	black pepper
2	lbs. beef	pinch of marjoram
2 to 3	cloves garlic	pinch of lovage
	salt	small quantity of water

Grind together pork meat with fat, beef, and garlic. Add remaining seasonings and a little water. Mix well. Fill into sausage casings, hang in a dry, cool place, and let remain overnight. Grill the next day.

Mititei

These homemade skinless sausages are a favorite among the Romanians. They are usually broiled outdoors on charcoal.

1 lb. rump beef	1/4 tsp. thyme
1 lb. breast beef	salt
3 or 4 cloves garlic	black pepper
1/4 tsp. baking soda	1/2 cup rich or concentrated
1/2 tsp. allspice	beef stock
1/4 tsp. ground cloves	

Trim meat, leaving some fat. Grind together with garlic. Place meat in bowl, and add baking soda and seasonings. Mix together with your hands. Slowly add beef stock and continue mixing, adding a little beef fat if necessary. When thoroughly mixed, roll meat in your palms into sausages 3½ inches long and 1 inch thick. Keep your palms wet so that the sausages will be smooth surfaced. Place sausages on platter, and keep in a dry, cool place overnight so that the flavors become well blended. Before cooking, keep them in a dry, cool place for 1 to 2 hours. Do not pierce sausages when cooking, so that none of the juice is lost.

Romanian Beef Sausage

5 lbs. coarse-ground beef chuck	5 cloves garlic, pressed
5 tsp. salt	1 tbsp. baking soda
1 tsp. black pepper	1½ tsp. cloves
	2 tbsp. sugar

Combine all ingredients, and mix well. Stuff into hog casings.

Romanian Pork and Beef Sausage

3 lbs. medium-ground pork butt	1/2 tsp. lovage
2 lbs. medium-ground beef chuck	11/2 tbsp. salt
6 cloves garlic, pressed	2 tsp. black pepper
	1/2 tsp. marjoram
	1 cup water

Combine all ingredients, and mix well. Stuff into hog casings.
Broil or bake.

RUSSIA

Russian Sausage

5 lbs. coarse-ground pork butt	3 tbsp. dill seed
2 large onions, chopped	3 tbsp. caraway seed
2 tbsp. pressed garlic	1 tbsp. black pepper
1 cup fresh parsley, chopped	1 tbsp. salt
	2 cups water

Combine all ingredients, and mix well. Stuff into hog casings. Bake for 1 hour.

SPAIN

From Spain came the chorizos, a very delicious variety of sausage that is a staple in many Spanish dishes. These little red sausages made from pork and highly flavored with red pepper are found wherever Spanish is spoken.

This Spanish sausage has a flavor all its own. If you have a smoke oven, you can smoke the links slowly to develop their spicy flavor. They will then keep for several weeks.

In the following recipes, you may use more or less hot pepper than the recommended amounts, for a hotter or milder sausage.

Chorizos #1

2½ lbs. lean pork	1 tbsp. wine vinegar
¾ lb. pork fat	½ tbsp. salt
2 fresh red peppers, seeded and sliced	1 tsp Spanish paprika
1 clove garlic, crushed	½ tsp. chili powder
⅓ cup red wine	¼ tsp. dried hot red pepper, crushed

Grind meat, fat, and fresh peppers with coarse blade. Add remaining ingredients. Wash eight 12-inch-long, 1⅛-inch-wide casings thoroughly. Stuff, tying off 10-inch sausage lengths.

Chorizos #2

2 lbs. coarse-ground pork, some fat
¼ cup vinegar
¼ cup olive oil
4 cloves garlic, minced
2 tbsp. paprika
3 tsp. salt
½ tsp. freshly ground black pepper
¼ tsp. sage
¼ cumin

Combine pork with vinegar, oil, garlic, and seasonings. Blend thoroughly. Force into sausage casings, pressing as tight as possible. Hang suspended in smoke oven for 24 hours over low heat.

Chorizos #3

2½ lbs. boneless fat pork
2 cloves garlic, minced
¾ cup chopped onions
2 tsp. salt
¾ tsp. freshly ground black pepper
2 tsp. Spanish paprika
½ tsp. dried ground chili peppers
1 tsp. cumin

Grind pork with a good layer of fat once. Then grind all ingredients together in food chopper. Fill sausage casings with mixture, or form into firm sausage shapes. Wrap sausages, and store in coldest portion of refrigerator. When ready to use, cook over very low heat until cooked through.

Chorizos #4

10 lbs. boneless pork butt	8 large cloves garlic
6 tbsp. salt	1 tbsp. oregano
1 cup vinegar	2 tsp. coarse black pepper
5 tbsp. paprika	1 cup water
3 tbsp. ground hot pepper	

Grind pork through ¼-inch plate, and place into mixer. Combine all other ingredients, and mix well until spices are evenly distributed. Stuff into 40- to 42-millimeter hog casings. Place on smoke sticks, and let dry in cooler overnight. This sausage takes much longer to dry than most.

Chorizos #5

1 lb. coarse-ground lean pork	1 tbsp. paprika
1 tsp. salt	1 clove garlic, crushed
2 tbsp. chili powder	1 tsp. oregano
¼ tsp. ground cloves	2 tbsp. vinegar
½ tsp. cinnamon	2 tbsp. water

Combine all ingredients, and mix well. Stuff in casings or cook as is. This sausage is best in casings.

Chorizos #6

35 lbs. pork trimmings (85% lean)	6 oz. chili powder
35 lbs. regular pork trimmings	2 oz. sodium nitrate
	2 lbs, 8 oz. salt
30 lbs. neck-bone trimmings	6 oz. sweet red peppers
8 oz. sugar	2 oz. hot red pepper
	1/4 oz. garlic powder

Chill pork trimmings and grind through 1/4-inch plate. Mix in mixer with sodium nitrate and seasonings. Stuff into 24- to 26-millimeter natural or collagen casings or into size 27 cellulose casings. Link at 4-inch intervals. You may package the sausage at this stage as fresh chorizo, dry it at 54 to 58 degrees for 10 days, or lightly smoke and dry it for 15 to 20 days at 55 to 58 degrees. The product is sometimes packaged in lard.

Chorizos #7

---

  50 lbs. coarse-ground pork with some fat
   ½ lb. Worcester salt
3 to 4 lbs. dried sweet red peppers (choriceros)
   ½ lb. fresh garlic

Mix pork and Worcester salt. Remove seeds from peppers, and put
in large container. Cover with cold water, and soak for 24 hours,
changing water often, until pulp can be scraped from skin. Put
through sieve or mill to remove skin, then add pulp to meat.

Grind garlic, and put in three small cheese bags. Squeeze juice
from bags onto meat, and stir well. Place bags in meat, and keep
mixture in cool place. Stir meat two or three times a day for 2 days.
Remove bags from meat mixture. Soak medium hog casings, then
stuff with hand grinder set at coarse. Crank meat through grinder
and through an adapter tube into casings. Tie sausages every
6 inches, or as long as you desire. Makes about 250 sausages.

Hang sausages over poles or rods in a well-ventilated, warm,
dry place. When sausage is dry and fairly hard, after about 5 days,
store in oil in a cool place. Alternatively, boil pork fat into pure
lard, put sausages into container, and fill container with melted
lard. Then store container. The lard will harden and can be used
for cooking grease.

The Basque Club of Ontario, Oregon, gave me this recipe.

Salchicha Extremena
Extremena Sausage

- 1 part lean pork
- 1 part liver
- 1 part tocino (fat bacon)
  - wild marjoram
  - anise

Place meats over low fire, along with wild marjoram and anise. When evenly browned, mince and mix well, then stuff into narrow intestine.

In Spain, tocino is the skin and fat from any part of the pig.

Salchichas Caseras con Trufas
Pork and Truffle Sausage

- 1 lb. lean pork
- 2 oz. bacon
- 2 oz. ham
- ½ lb. mushrooms
- 1¼ cups brandy or rum seasoning
- a few truffles, sliced
- 2 tbsp. lard, melted
- 3 oz. bread crumbs
- 2 oz. parsley, chopped

Put pork, mushrooms, bacon, and ham through grinder twice. Add brandy or rum seasoning, and mix well. Wash pig intestine, rinse well, and leave in warm water to keep flexible. When ready to stuff, press water out of intestine and fill with pork mixture, putting in a slice of truffle now and then. You may leave in a long piece or cut into individual sausages, but be sure to secure ends. Brush sausages with melted lard, and dip in mixed bread crumbs and parsley.

Spanish Mortadella

35	lbs. lean pork, cured	1	oz. juniper berries, crushed
10	lbs. choice beef, cured	1	oz. garlic compound
5	lbs. pork fat, cured		flour
$1/16$	lb. coriander	4	oz. sugar
$1/16$	lb. cloves	$1/4$	oz. Spanish sausage
$1/4$	lb. summer sausage		seasoning
	seasoning	$1/2$	oz. rum flavor

Cut fat into $1/4$-inch pieces. Run each lot of meat through meat grinder separately, and then finish in silent cutter. Mix meat and fat together, and add remaining ingredients, including enough flour to reach desired consistency. When well mixed, spread about 5 inches think on clean boards, and place in cooler for 24 hours at 38 to 40 degrees.

Stuff into small and medium-size beef bladders. Prick with a needle, and tie crosswise with heavy cord. Put same-size pieces on separate sticks, and hang in cooler at 38 to 40 degrees for 24 hours. Then hang in steam room, and turn on steam for drying. During the first 4 hours, use very little steam and work up to 120 degrees. Keep room at 120 degrees for 10 hours, then allow temperature to rise gradually to 145 degrees over the next 5 to 6 hours. Keep room at 145 degrees for 4 to 5 hours. After sausage has been in steam room for 24 to 30 hours, cut a small sausage to the center to see if it is done. When sausages are done, remove from steam room. Sausages need to sweat and cool slowly, and they must be covered with cloths so that they do not dry and cool too quickly.

SWEDEN

Sausage making has been a Swedish tradition for many centuries. It is likely that the Goths, and later the Vikings, starting about 800 A.D., took some type of preserved meat on their long voyages. These were probably chopped meats, cured with salt, stuffed into reindeer casings, smoked, and dry cured. It is also likely that these early seafaring Scandinavians brought home with them sausage-making knowledge from Greece and the Roman Empire.

With Sweden's cooler climate a major part of the year, refrigeration is not a problem, and most Swedish sausages are soft varieties, rather than the hard, long-keeping types of the warmer southern Europe and Mediterranean area, and are not very highly seasoned.

Potatiskorv #1
Swedish Potato Sausage

1 lb. boneless beef	½ cup cold water
1 lb. boneless veal	7 tsp. salt
1 lb. boneless pork shoulder	½ tsp. allspice
1½ lbs. baking potatoes, pared	¼ tsp. white pepper
2 medium onions	¼ tsp. black pepper

Put meats, potatoes, and onions through food chopper once. Add remaining ingredients, and mix well. Cut ½ pound sausage casings into desired lengths, and stuff with sausage mixture. To cook, cover sausage with boiling water. Bring slowly to a simmer, cover, and simmer 45 minutes. Carefully remove from water to platter. Cut into 2-inch lengths for serving. For the best flavor, potato sausage should not be frozen, as raw potatoes do not freeze well.

Potatiskorv #2

1 lb. lean ground beef	1 onion, finely chopped
½ lb. lean ground pork	1 tbsp. salt
7 cups grated potatoes	2 tsp. ground ginger

Mix all ingredients together, and stuff loosely into sausage casings. Sausages should be about 5 inches long. Cover sausages with salted water, and refrigerate until ready to use. To cook, remove sausages from brine, and poach in salted water for ½ hour. Drain. Melt ⅓ cup butter in large skillet, and brown sausages on all sides.

Flaskkorv
Pork Sausage

1 lb. pork fat	1 tsp. coarsely ground allspice
2 lbs. lean pork	1 tsp. ground ginger
1 lb. lean beef	1/2 tsp. ground cloves
1 lb. potatoes, peeled	1/2 tsp. saltpeter
1/2 cup potato flour	5 cups milk or pork stock
5 tsp. salt	Cure: 4 tbsp. salt, 2 tbsp.
1 1/2 tsp. black pepper	sugar, 1 tsp. saltpeter

Have your butcher grind half the amount of pork fat with lean pork and beef three times. Dice remaining pork fat very small. Cook potatoes 12 minutes or until half done. Pour off water, and shake pan over heat to dry them. Cool overnight, then mash thoroughly or put through meat grinder. Place all ingredients except liquid and cure in large bowl. Work with your hands, slowly adding liquid until mixture has the consistency of fairly thick porridge (this takes about 50 minutes). If desired, you may check seasonings by boiling a small amount of sausage mixture in lightly salted water for 25 to 30 minutes.

Cut 6 yards fairly narrow (about 3 inches wide) round or straight casings into desired lengths. Tie each length at one end and fill loosely, then tie other ends. Rinse sausages under cold running water, and drain on towel. Combine curing ingredients, and rub on sausages. Store in large bowl in cold place.

This sausage is best when eaten within a few days. If it has to be kept longer, place in cold brine. Makes about 8 sausages.

Smoked Christmas Sausage

2½ lbs. beef top round
2½ lbs. lean pork
2½ lbs. pork fat
2½ lbs. peeled potatoes
2 tbsp. salt
1 tsp. saltpeter

2 tsp. coarsely ground black pepper
1 qt. milk
⅓ cup brandy
Cure: 3 tbsp. salt, 1 tbsp. sugar, 1½ tsp. saltpeter

Grind beef three times, the last two times together with lean pork. Dice pork fat into small cubes. Boil potatoes 12 minutes or until half cooked; pour off water. Cool overnight, then put through meat grinder. Place all ingredients except liquids and cure into large bowl. Work with your hands, slowly adding liquids for 1 hour or until mixture has porous but firm consistency.

Cut 4 yards of 3-inch-wide straight casings into desired lengths. Tie each length at one end, and stuff mixture into casings with horn or sausage filler attached to meat grinder. This kind of sausage must be stuffed as hard as possible. Prick any air bubbles with a pin, and press out air. When stuffed, tie other ends.

Rinse sausages under cold running water; drain on towels. Combine curing ingredients, and rub on sausages. Cold smoke for 6 days. Makes about 8 medium-size sausages.

Gasleverkorv
Goose Liver Sausage

1 goose liver	1 tsp. salt
2 tbsp. rice	½ tbsp. finely chopped
1 cup milk	onion
1 tbsp. raisins	½ tbsp. butter
¼ tsp. marjoram	1 egg yolk (or whole
¼ tsp. white pepper	small egg)

Scald rice, boil in milk until soft, and leave to cool. Lightly brown onion in butter, and scald raisins. Pound liver, pass through wire sieve, and mix with raisins, seasonings, and onion. Stir in egg yolk.

If you have a whole goose and want to make authentic casing, roll skin off neck of a goose before roasting. Clean well, and sew up at one end. Stuff three-quarters full with sausage meat, and sew up other ends. You can also use regular sausage skins. Simmer the sausages in salted water, uncovered for ½ hours, together with giblets. When cold, cut into slices.

Varmlandskorv
Varmland Sausage

2 lbs. pork, boned
2 lbs. beef, boned
2 lbs. raw potatoes
3 onions
1 to 2 tbsp. salt
$\frac{1}{4}$ tsp. white pepper

$\frac{1}{2}$ tsp. allspice
$2\frac{1}{4}$ cups water or
ham stock
Cure: 4 tbsp. salt, 2 tbsp.
sugar, 1 tsp. saltpeter

Cut meats into pieces. Mince two or three times, the last time with potatoes and onions. Add seasonings, and mix well. Moisten carefully with liquid, and work mixture thoroughly. Cook a test sample to check seasonings and consistency. If mixture is too stiff, moisten with more liquid; if too soft, add a little potato flour.

Fill 4 yards curved sausage casings very loosely, and knot into links. Cool in cold water, then dry. Combine curing ingredients, rub on sausages, and leave them overnight. Sausages may be kept for several days in brine.

Brine (Saltlake). To each $4\frac{1}{2}$ cups water, add 4 ounces ($\frac{1}{2}$ cup) coarse salt and 1 tablespoon sugar. Bring to a boil. Skim, and leave brine to cool.

Brackkorv
Polony

---

2 lbs. beef, boned	1 tsp. white pepper
2 lbs. lean pork, boned	1/2 tsp. allspice
1 lb. fat bacon, in one piece	3 1/4 to scant 4 1/2 cups
1 lb. fat bacon, in small cubes	boiled, cold milk
2 potatoes, boiled	Cure: 4 tbsp. salt,
2 tbsp. salt	2 tbsp. sugar,
1 tbsp. sugar	1 1/2 tsp. saltpeter
1 tsp. saltpeter	

Cut meats into pieces. Mince with whole piece of fat bacon two or three times, the last time together with potatoes. Add seasonings, moisten carefully with milk, and work mixture very thoroughly. Stir in cubes of fat bacon. Fry a test sample, and check for seasonings.

Fill 4 yards straight sausage casings firmly, and knot into links. Cool in cold water, then dry. Combine curing ingredients, rub on sausages, and leave them overnight. Squeeze contents together firmly if they are too loose, and retie.

These sausages are suitable for smoking. If you wish to do so, halve the amounts of salt and pepper called for, since the flavor gets stronger through the smoking procedure. Smoke sausages in warm smokehouse for half a day. Hang in cold place to store.

Medvurst
Mettwurst

---

2 lbs. beef, boned	scant ½ tsp. ground cloves
2 lbs. lean pork, boned	7 tbsp. water or stock
2 lbs. fat bacon	7 tbsp. brandy
2 tbsp. salt	Cure: 4 tbsp. salt,
1 tsp. saltpeter	2 tbsp. sugar,
1 to 2 tsp. white pepper	½ tsp. saltpeter

Cut meats into pieces, and mince two or three times. Cut fat bacon into small cubes. Add seasonings to minced meats, moisten carefully with liquids, and work mixture thoroughly. Stir in cubes of fat bacon. Fry a test sample, and check for seasonings.

Pack 3 yards straight sausage casings tightly with mixture, and knot into links. Cool in cold water, then dry. Combine curing ingredients, rub on sausages, and leave them in a cold place for 2 days. Turn sausages a couple of times during this period, and at the same time rub any brine that has formed onto sausages. Squeeze sausages together tightly, and retie. These sausages are suitable for smoking.

Leverkorv
Liver Sausage

---

2 lbs. ox or pork liver	scant ½ tsp. white pepper
1 lb. boneless veal	marjoram
½ lb. fat bacon	2¼ cups boiled, cold milk
2 tbsp. chopped onion, fried	1 tbsp. salt

Wash liver, and steep in cold water for a few hours if desired. Mince and sieve liver. Mince meat two or three times, the last time together with fat bacon. Mix liver with meat and fat bacon, add onion and seasonings, and work mixture thoroughly. Moisten carefully with milk. Fry a sample, and check for seasonings.

Fill 2 yards straight sausage casings fairly loosely, and tie up sausages. Wash in cold water. Place in saucepan and cover with water. Add 2 teaspoons salt for each 4½ cups water. Simmer sausages very carefully uncovered for about 30 minutes. Allow sausages to cool before cutting up.

Goteborg
Swedish Sausage

60 lbs. beef trimmings, cured	salt
30 lbs. pork trimmings, cured	½ lb. sugar
10 lbs. pork back fat, cured	1 oz. finely ground cardamon
1 lb. summer sausage seasoning	flour

Mix meats and fat, and run through ⅛-inch plate of grinder. Place in mixer, and add remaining ingredients, including enough flour for proper consistency. Spread mixture 5 to 6 inches thick on boards, and place in cooler at 38 to 40 degrees for 2 days. Then taken out of cooler and mix again. Stuff into 14- to 18-inch-long beef middles. Place into vats and cover with brine testing at 80 degrees by the salinometer. Keep at a temperature of 40 degrees for 2 to 3 days, then rinse with water and put in smokehouse. Cold smoke for about 3 days.

SWITZERLAND

Switzerland is a country of several different languages and cultures, and there is a great variety of sausages produced. These differ according to climate and culture.

In the German part of Switzerland, mostly scalded (cooked) sausage products are found. In the French part, raw or smoked link sausages are most common. In the very favorable climate of the mountain cantons, which partly belong to the Romanisch and the Italian-speaking sector, air-dried summer sausages are produced, and in the exclusive Italian speaking Canton Teassin region are found, as in northern Italy, durable sausage products suitable for southern climates.

Switzerland is a sausage-eating country par excellence. There are any number of superb sausages made from beef, veal, and pork, prepared in local communities or marketed nationally as ready-to-cook sausage. Their composition and spicing are often the secret of their makers. Suffice it to say that a good sausage has made many a Swiss butcher rich and famous.

Swiss Bauerwurst
Smoked Sausage

3 lbs. fine-ground beef chuck	1 tsp. allspice
2 lbs. fine-ground pork butt	1½ cups cream
5 tsp. salt	1 cup water
5 tsp. caraway seed	

Combine all ingredients, and mix well. Stuff into hog casings. Sprinkle with equal parts salt and brown sugar. Refrigerate overnight. Hot smoke about 3 hours, or bake until done.

Swiss Bratwurst (Weisswurst)
White Sausages

Traditional bratwurst sausages are a favorite of the Swiss.

30 lbs. lean young pork trimmings	³/₄ lb. German pork sausage seasoning
40 lbs. veal trimmings	¹/₂ lemon rind, chopped
10 lbs. young pork fat	1¹/₂ lbs. salt
2 gal. sweet milk	flour

Trim meats and fat carefully, and chop very fine or grind with ⁵/₆₄-inch plate on meat grinder. Mix milk with ground meat, and gradually add remaining ingredients, including enough flour for proper consistency. Stuff loosely into thin hog casings, and twist into 3¹/₂- to 4-inch links. Will keep in refrigerator for 3 to 4 days. Must be cooked before serving.

Scandinavian Sausage

2¹/₂ lbs. fine-ground veal	1 tsp. black pepper
2¹/₂ lbs. fine-ground pork	1 tsp. ground ginger
2 large potatoes, mashed	1¹/₂ tsp. allspice
6 tsp. salt	2 cups milk
2 tsp. sugar	

Combine all ingredients, and mix well. Stuff into hog casings. Sprinkle with equal parts salt and brown sugar. Refrigerate overnight. Smoke for 3 to 4 hours, or scald and brown.

UKRAINE

Sausage is a very important part of the Ukrainian food culture. Most native Ukrainian sausages show the influence of the surrounding countries. The Slavic countries in Eastern Europe share a common heritage of garlicky beef and pork sausages similar to the Polish kielbasa.

Ukrainian Sausage

A traditional Ukrainian sausage is made from the choice cuts of pork with a small amount of fat. Some cooks use a mixture of two-thirds pork and one-third veal for a superior product. For quick use, the sausage is not smoked, but baked fresh. It is a delicious dish.

      2 lbs. or more pork loin
      1 clove garlic, crushed
         salt
         black pepper
    ½ cup water

Remove bones and skin from meat, but retain fat. Cut meat and fat into very small pieces; do not grind. Add other ingredients, and mix with your hands until thoroughly blended. Stuff mixture into sausage casings, leaving no empty spaces, and tie ends with string. Prick entire length of sausages with a needle to let out any air. Sausage is now ready for smoking or baking. Bake in greased roaster, uncovered, at 350 degrees for about 1 hour, or until delicately browned and cooked through. If you wish, you can add enough water to barely cover sausage before baking, and save drippings to use for sauerkraut dishes.

Saltseson

Here is an old-country specialty that is worth reviving. It is made of a variety of pork meats formed into a pressed loaf. When properly prepared, saltseson is a great delicacy and a favorite as an appetizer. It is quite a lot of trouble to make, but it is worth the effort.

2	pork ears	1	medium onion, quartered
1	pork heart	1	medium carrot, quartered
1	pork tongue	1	bay leaf
2	pork kidneys	8	peppercorns
½	lb. fat pork shoulder	2	tbsp. salt
1	lb. pork liver	1	clove garlic
1	pork stomach	½	tsp. saltpeter
1	cup fresh pig or		
	calf blood, strained		

Singe, scrape, and wash pork ears very thoroughly. Cut heart into halves, remove veins and arteries, and wash well under running water. Cut away roots from tongue, scrub, skin, and wash well. Split kidneys into halves, remove fat and tubes, and wash thoroughly under running water. Cut pork shoulder into several pieces. Place all of these in large kettle, cover with cold water, and bring to a boil. Skim, then add vegetables and seasonings. Cover and simmer until meat is tender.

When done, add liver and saltpeter. Continue cooking a while longer until liver is done. Strain meat, reserving stock. Remove all vegetables, spices, and bones from meat. Cut meat into small pieces. Do not discard ear gristle; chop it into small bits. Finely chop skin and fat from pork shoulder. Crush garlic and add to 2 cups of hot stock. Strain stock and pour over meat. Season to taste with salt and pepper. Then add blood and mix thoroughly.

Have pork stomach cleaned and washed. Most meat markets sell this organ cleaned and prepared to use. Fill stomach three-quarters full with meat mixture, and sew edges securely. It is very important that you do not overfill. Place in large kettle, cover with hot water, and simmer, covered, for 30 to 40 minutes. Test for readiness by pricking with darning needle. If juice is clear with no blood coloring, meat is ready.

When done, remove saltseson to plate and let cool slightly. To flatten loaf and give it a uniform shape, place a board over loaf and weight down with a light weight. Be careful about the weight; it must not be too heavy or the loaf will crack. A brick may serve the purpose. Chill thoroughly. Before serving, remove meat from stomach casing and cut into slices. Saltseson keeps well when refrigerated.

Ukrainian Beef and Pork Sausage

1½ lbs. beef chuck	1 tsp. marjoram
¼ lb. beef plate or other fatty cut of beef	2 tsp. mustard seed
	½ tsp. coriander
1 lb. pork butt	½ tsp. ground ginger
½ lb. smoked bacon	2 tsp. kosher salt
1 tsp. coarse-ground pepper	1 tsp. curing salt (optional)
1 tbsp. sweet Hungarian paprika	2 tsp. sugar
2 tbsp. cracked black pepper	½ cup water
	1 tbsp. chopped garlic

Grind beef through ⅜-inch plate, and pork and bacon through ¼-inch plate. Mix ground meats and all remaining ingredients in large bowl. Knead until well blended. Stuff into medium or wide hog casings. If you are using curing salts and intend to cold smoke sausages, air-dry them overnight in front of a fan, then cold smoke for 12 to 24 hours. Otherwise, hot smoke to an internal temperature of 155 degrees. You can also leave sausages raw and unsmoked. The raw sausage will keep for 3 days refrigerated, smoked versions up to 1 week, and frozen sausages for 2 months.

Kyshka with Buckwheat and Blood Stuffing

Some meat dealers who specialize in European products feature this old-fashioned sausage ready-cooked, but a homemade one is far superior. For a richer flavor, cook buckwheat groats in soup stock instead of water.

2 cups buckwheat groats	salt
8 cups water	black pepper
4 tbsp. lard	1 cup fresh pig or calf blood

Stir groats into rapidly boiling water, and add lard and seasonings. Cook over high heat, stirring a few times, until mixture thickens. Remove from heat. Taste critically for seasoning, and add more if necessary. Cool slightly. Strain blood, and combine with buckwheat. This mixture should not be too thick. While still warm, fill sausage casing three-quarters full, and tie ends securely with string. Do not overfill. Place sausage in greased baking pan, and either brush with melted fat or add enough water to barely cover. Bake, uncovered, at 350 degrees for about 1½ hours or until done. When partially cooked, prick sausage in several places with a needle to prevent cracking. Remove when done, and serve hot.

Kyshka keeps well when refrigerated. Reheat whole, or brown slices on both sides in hot butter.

UNITED STATES

The earliest Americans, the Indians, chopped meat, mixed it with meal, herbs, and berries, and stuffed it into bags made of skin. The mixture, though crude, would keep well enough to provide food for the cold winters when fresh meat was scarce. American sausage making as we know it today, however, has developed only within the past one hundred years, and every region has its own favorites.

Oyster and Pork Sausage

Sausage and oysters might sound like an odd combination, but the salty tang of the oyster and the spice of the sausage go together beautifully.

1½ cups chucked fresh oysters (or 12 oz. jar)	½ tsp. black pepper
½ lb. pork shoulder	2 tsp. kosher salt
½ beef suet	½ tsp. dried thyme
2 cups fresh white bread crumbs	⅛ tsp. allspice
2 tsp. fresh lemon juice	¼ tsp. nutmeg
	½ tsp. Tabasco

Grind oysters and beef suet through ¼-inch plate. In large bowl, mix together all ingredients. Fry a small amount of mixture, and check for seasonings. Stuff into medium hog casings, and tie into 5-inch lengths. Prick sausages, and poach in simmering 180-degree salted water for 10 to 15 minutes, until firm. Cool. Fry in 2 tablespoons of butter or 1 tablespoon of peanut oil. Makes 2 to 3 pounds.

New England Pressed Sausage

90 lbs. lean shoulder pork
10 lbs. beef trimmings
   Cure: 1 lb. pickle cure, 1 lb. sugar, 2 lbs. salt

First you must cure meats. It is absolutely necessary that meats be thoroughly chilled and that packing be done in a cooler so that temperature in which meats will be cured is correct, 38 to 40 degrees. Cut meat into same-size pieces to ensure even curing. Mix curing ingredients, and sprinkle onto meat.

Have curing barrels clean and sweet, sprinkle a little salt on bottom, and fill about one-quarter full of salted meat. Pound down with tamper. Fill to the halfway point, tamp again, and continue in this manner until barrels are full. Tamping removes any air between pieces of meat.

Cover meat with a piece of parchment paper, put a piece of cheesecloth over this, and spread a layer of salt 2 or 3 inches thick over cloth. Fold in overhanging edges. This will keep out air and give good results. Salt and cheesecloth may be used again in the future. Meats will be cured in 2 or 3 weeks.

To make sausage, run beef trimmings through $5/64$-inch plate of meat grinder. Mix with ground cured pork. When thoroughly mixed, stuff into 12- to 14-inch-long beef bungs. Wrap with heavy twine or ham cord at intervals of 2 to 3 inches. Smoke for 3 hours. Cool at a temperature of 155 degrees for 2 to 3 hours. Lay sausages on boards in cooler, and put another board on top with heavy weights to press them. After they are cooled, hang in cooler or refrigerator overnight, then smoke again for 8 to 10 hours. When cooled they are ready to serve.

Spicy Hot Italian Sausage

This spicy sausage is the one you're likely to find sizzling on a grill at a lunch counter in New York City's Little Italy.

³⁄₄ lbs. pork butt	1 tbsp. red pepper flakes
³⁄₄ lb. pork back fat	2 tsp. ground black pepper
1 tbsp. minced garlic	2 tbsp. anise-flavored
4 tbsp. kosher salt	liqueur, such as
2 tbsp. anise or fennel seed	Sambuca
1 tsp. cayenne	¹⁄₄ cup cold water

Combine ingredients except water in large bowl. Grind everything together through ³⁄₈-inch plate. Moisten with water, squeeze, and knead mixture until everything is well blended. Stuff into medium hog casings, and tie into 5-inch lengths.

Lebanon Bologna

Lebanon bologna is traditionally made under conditions that call for little or no refrigeration. The finished product is very stable.

10	lbs. beef	$\frac{1}{2}$ tsp. white pepper	
2	oz. salt	$\frac{1}{2}$ tsp. ginger	
1	oz sugar	$\frac{1}{2}$ tsp. mace	
1	tsp. dry mustard	$\frac{1}{2}$ tsp. sodium nitrate	

Salt meat and hold for 8 to 10 days at 34 to 38 degrees. Grind beef through $\frac{1}{2}$-inch plate, and mix in ribbon mixer with other ingredients. Pass mixture through $\frac{1}{8}$-inch plate, and stuff into No. 8 fibrous casings. Tie and stockinette filled casings for support. Smoke for 4 to 7 days with cold smoke, usually 4 days in summer and 7 days in late fall and winter months.

Lebanon Bologna in Bulk

100	lbs. whole carcass cow meat	2	oz. white pepper
1 lb., 8 oz.	salt	1	oz. ginger
1	lb. sugar	1	oz. mace
8	oz. dry mustard	1	oz. sodium nitrate

Salt whole carcass cow meat with 2 percent salt, and hold for 8 to 10 days at 34 to 38 degrees. Grind beef through $\frac{1}{2}$-inch plate, and mix in ribbon mixer with other ingredients. Pass mixture through $\frac{1}{8}$-inch plate, and stuff into No. 8 fibrous casings. Tie, stockinette, and smoke same as Lebanon Bologna.

Old Maryland Sausages

10	lbs. fresh pork (20% fat)	4	tbsp. salt
2	tbsp. ground pepper	5	tbsp. crumbled sage
³/₄	tsp. cayenne	¹/₂	tsp. saltpeter

Combine seasonings. Cut pork into pieces, and grind very fine. Mix with seasonings. Stuff into casings.

Country Ham and Pork Sausage

Country ham is one of the delights of Southern cooking. The hams from Smithfield County in Virginia have the greatest reputation and are widely available. They have a smoky and pungent aroma and a special flavor that is reputed to come from the peanuts the hogs feed on. If you have a whole ham, this recipe gives you a good way to use the trimmed fat and any leftover meat.

2	lbs. pork butt	¹/₂	tsp. ground ginger
¹/₂ to ³/₄	leftover boiled or	¹/₄	tsp. ground cloves
	baked ham	¹/₂	tsp. sage
¹/₂	lb. fat from ham	1	tsp. black pepper
¹/₂	lb. fresh pork back fat	1	tsp. red pepper flakes
2	oz. ham skin (optional)	³/₄ to 1	cup water
1	tsp. sugar		

Grind pork butt through ³/₈-inch plate, and the ham, ham fat, pork back fat, and skin through ¹/₈-inch plate. If you are starting out with raw country ham, simmer a ³/₄-pound piece for about 2 hours and cool before grinding. (The ham stock can be used for pea or bean soup. Taste to make sure it's not too salty.) Combine all ingredients, and mix well. Stuff into medium hog casings, and tie into 5-inch links.

Norfolk Sausage

5 lbs. medium-ground beef chuck	1½ tbsp. black pepper
1 small onion, grated	1 tbsp. basil
8 cloves garlic, pressed	1 tbsp. oregano
2 cups grated Parmesan	2 tsp. mustard seed
1½ tbsp. salt	1½ cups red wine

Combine all ingredients, mix well, and stuff into hog casings. Bake or broil.

Spicy Fresh Country Sausage

3 lbs. pork butt	1 tsp. thyme
¾ to 1 lb. pork back fat	2 tsp. sugar
4 tsp. kosher salt	1 tbsp. red pepper flakes
2 tsp. black pepper	1 tsp. cayenne
2 tsp. sage	½ cup water

Put meat and fat through ¼-inch plate of meat grinder. Combine all ingredients in large bowl, kneading and squeezing meat until everything is blended. Stuff meat into medium hog casings and tie into 4-inch links, or keep in bulk form.

Kentucky-Style Pork Sausage

Here is a variation of Spicy Fresh Country Sausage that you might find in Kentucky. This sausage is usually in bulk but can be stuffed into casings if desired.

2 lbs. pork butt	1 tsp. cayenne
1 lb. pork back fat	1 tsp. coriander
1 tbsp. kosher salt	1/2 tsp. freshly grated nutmeg
2 tsp. black pepper	1/2 cup cold water
2 tsp. sage	

Grind pork and fat through 1/4-inch plate. Mix all ingredients together, kneading and squeezing until blended. For links, stuff into medium hog casings and tie into 5-inch lengths.

Tennessee Sausage

Where there was an oversupply at hog-killing time, an old Tennessee country custom was to bake or fry large quantities of sausage cakes, pack them down in jars, and cover with fresh pure melted lard. This preserved the meat for weeks.

2 lbs. pork fat	1 tbsp. black pepper
3 1/2 lbs. lean pork	1 tsp. cayenne
1 cup powdered sage	pinch of thyme
1 tbsp. red pepper	12 cloves, powdered
1 tbsp. salt	12 allspice, powdered
1 blade mace, powdered	

Grind meat and fat together. Combine seasonings, and work thoroughly through ground meat. Form into small cakes ready to fry or bake, or fill into casings and smoke or use fresh.

Herbed Fresh Sausage Plantation-Style

This recipe is typical of the mild and aromatic style of sausage that was found in plantation kitchens. The flavor is more delicate and complex than that of the Spicy Fresh Country Sausage, without its bite of cayenne and red pepper but with a lovely perfume from the herbs and spices. The bread crumbs give the sausage a softer texture.

1 lb. pork butt	³/₄ tsp. marjoram
1 lb. veal shoulder	³/₄ tsp. thyme
³/₄ lb. pork back fat	¹/₄ tsp. summer savory
1 cup day-old bread crumbs	1 tsp. sage
2 tbsp. grated lemon zest	¹/₂ tsp. mace
1 tbsp. kosher salt	¹/₂ cup cold water
1¹/₂ tsp. black pepper	

Put meats and fat through ¹/₄-inch plate of meat grinder. Mix in bread crumbs, lemon zest, and seasonings. Chill mixture for about ¹/₂ hour, and grind again. Add water, and knead and squeeze until well mixed. Stuff into sheep or medium hog casings and tie into 4-inch links, or leave sausage in bulk and fry patties as needed. Keeps 2 months frozen. Makes 3 to 4 pounds.

Country-Style Sausage

2 lbs. coarse-ground fresh
    lean pork
1 tsp. salt
¼ tsp. freshly ground
    black pepper
½ tsp. thyme or sage
    dash cayenne

Combine all ingredients, and mix well with your hands. Divide in half and shape into two rolls, wrapping each securely in foil. Sausage will keep for several weeks under refrigeration.

Lamb Breakfast Sausage

1 lb. lean ground lamb
⅓ lb. ground pork
    (or use all lamb)
⅛ tsp. coarse-ground
    black pepper
½ tsp. salt
¼ tsp. marjoram
¼ tsp. thyme
¼ to ½ tsp. sage

Crush dried herbs to a powder. (Poultry seasoning or all sage may be used instead.) Add pork to lamb if desired, and add seasonings. Mix all ingredients together thoroughly. Cover bowl and place in refrigerator overnight. To serve, shape sausage meat into ½-inch-thick patties, and brown in skillet. Makes 6 to 7 servings.

Pork Sausage #1

10 lbs. chopped pork	6 tsp. salt
12 tsp. sage	2 tsp. cloves
6 tsp. black pepper	1 tsp. nutmeg

Combine all ingredients, and mix thoroughly. Pack in several separate containers, cover with waxed paper, and store in a cool place. It will keep for days.

Pork Sausage #2

20 lbs. dressed pork	1 tsp. ground ginger
10 lbs. clear fat pork	1/2 lb. fine salt
2 tsp. sugar	2 tbsp. black pepper
1 tbsp. sage (optional)	

Cut meat into small pieces, and add seasonings. Put through sausage cutter, grinding twice. Pack into sterilized jars, cover with 1/2 inch layer of lard, and keep in a cold place. Use as wanted.

Pork Sausage #3

---

3 lbs. fresh pork
  ($\frac{1}{2}$ fat, $\frac{1}{2}$ lean)
1 onion, finely chopped
  or ground
1 small clove garlic
1 tbsp. salt
1 tsp. coarsely ground
  black pepper

1 tsp. basil
1 tsp. crushed fennel seed
1 tsp. coriander
1 tsp. tarragon
$\frac{1}{4}$ tsp. ground ginger
1 tsp. monosodium
  glutamate

Grind pork to desired texture. Crush garlic to a paste, and add to meat along with onion and seasonings. Mix together well with your hands. Form into patties and fry.

Ozark Sausage

Ozark Sausage is something special, for those isolated hills still guard the pioneer cooking lore that has been passed down from previous generations.

30 lbs. pork ($\frac{3}{4}$ lean, $\frac{1}{4}$ fat)
1 cup salt
1 cup rubbed sage

$\frac{1}{2}$ cup black pepper
$\frac{1}{4}$ cup red pepper
1 tbsp. brown sugar

Cut pork into strips for grinding. Mix seasonings well with meat, then grind. You can stuff into casings or make into patties for frying.

Chaurice

It has been said by visitors to New Orleans that the Creoles surpass all other cooks in preparing appetizing sausages. Their high seasoning distinguishes Creole sausages from all others. Chaurice must be seasoned very hot, so do not fear having too much red pepper.

4 lbs. lean fresh pork	1 tsp. hot chili pepper
2 lbs. fat fresh pork	1 tsp. cayenne
2 large onions	1 tsp. red pepper
1 clove garlic	2 tsp. finely ground
3 tsp. salt	black pepper
3 sprigs parsley, minced	1 sprig thyme, minced
½ tsp. allspice, ground very fine	2 bay leaves, minced

Hash lean and fat pork as fine as possible, and mix together. Add dry seasonings. Mince onion, garlic, and herbs as fine as possible, add to mixture, and mix well. Clean casings (the Creoles use sheep entrails), scald them, and wash again. Dry and fill with mixture, tying them in the lengths you desire.

Saucisses à la Creole
Creole Sausage

1 lb. lean pork, ground	¼ tsp. ground chili pepper
½ lb. pork fat, ground	¼ tsp. cayenne
½ large onion, chopped fine	¼ tsp. dried thyme
½ garlic clove, crushed	¼ tsp. allspice
½ tsp. salt	small bay leaf, crumbled
½ tsp. freshly ground black pepper	1 tbsp. parsley

Combine all ingredients, and mix well. Shape into roll, wrap securely in foil, and refrigerate. Keeps well for several weeks.

Creole Pork Sausage

4 lbs. lean pork	3 tsp. salt
2 lbs. fat pork	2 tsp. black pepper
2 large onions	½ tsp. cayenne
1 clove garlic	½ tsp. chili pepper
1 sprig thyme	½ tsp. paprika
1 sprig parsley	½ tsp. allspice
2 bay leaves	

Grind pork as fine as possible, mixing fat and lean. Add salt, peppers, and paprika, and mix thoroughly. Mince onions, garlic, and herbs very fine, and add along with allspice. Clean sheep casings, scald them, and wash again. Dry and fill with sausage mixture. Tie in lengths to make about six to a pound.

Louisiana-Style Smoked Sausage

This spicy smoked sausage is a real favorite all over Louisiana.

1½ lbs. pork butt	¼ tsp. thyme
1 lb. beef chuck	¼ tsp. savory
½ lb. pork back fat	¼ tsp. sage
2 tsp. chopped garlic	pinch of allspice
1 tbsp. kosher salt	pinch of ground cloves
1 tbsp. black pepper	2 tsp. sugar
2 tsp. red pepper flakes	1½ tsp. curing salts
1 tsp. cayenne	½ cup ice water

Grind meats through ⅜-inch plate. Combine all ingredients, and blend well with your hands, kneading and squeezing mixture. Stuff mixture into medium hog casings, and twist off 6-inch lengths. Dry overnight at room temperature, then cold smoke. Cook before eating.

Cajun Boudin Noir
Spicy Blood Sausage

The boucherie, or pig killing, is one of the big events in the late fall all through the Cajun country of southwest Louisiana. Pig meat and sausage of every kind provide lots of good eating at these lively gatherings.

1½	lbs. pork butt	1	tsp. allspice
½	lb. pork back fat	1	tsp. mace
2½	cups hog or beef blood	3	tbsp. black pepper
2	onions, chopped	1	tbsp. fresh marjoram
2	tbsp. lard or vegetable oil	1	tsp. dried thyme
1½	cups cooked rice	2	tsp. cayenne
1	cup chopped parsley	1	tsp. red pepper flakes
5	tsp. salt	3	cloves garlic, minced

Grind meat and fat through ¼-inch plate. Sauté onions in lard in heavy skillet over medium heat until transparent. Mix together ground pork and cooked rice with blood and seasonings. Add onions, and stir to mix evenly. Tie off end of 10- to 12-foot length of medium hog casing, and stuff with mixture. It is best to work over large pan or plastic dishwashing tub, as things get a bit messy. Tie into 4- to 5-inch lengths.

Bring large pot of water to just below a simmer. Add sausages. Keep heat low, with water at about 180 degrees, so that sausages will not burst. Poach for 30 to 40 minutes, until you can prick sausages and no blood comes out, and the internal temperature reads 150 degrees. May be frozen for 2 months. Makes about 4 pounds.

Louisiana-Style Pork Sausage

2 lbs. lean pork	1 tsp. black pepper
1 lb. fresh side pork	1/4 tsp. thyme
1 medium onion, minced	1/2 tsp. cayenne
1 clove garlic, minced	1/2 tsp. chili pepper
3 tsp. salt	

Run pork through grinder using 3/16-inch plate. Add onion and garlic. Blend seasonings well, sprinkle over meat, and thoroughly mix. Stuff mixture into either sheep casings for small links or hog casings for large links, or shape into patties.

Spicy Pork and Veal Sausage

4 lbs. fine-ground pork butt	1 1/2 tsp. white pepper
1 lb. fine-ground veal	1/2 tsp. ground cloves
1 cup potato flour	1/2 tsp. ginger
2 tbsp. sugar	4 cups water
2 tbsp. salt	

Combine all ingredients, and mix well. Stuff into hog casings. Sprinkle with equal parts salt and sugar. Refrigerate for 24 hours. Poach about 20 minutes, then broil or fry.

Sheboygan Brats
Fresh Farm Bratwurst

Folks in the Midwest take their bratwurst very seriously, especially in Wisconsin around Sheboygan, home of the annual Bratwurst Festival. There, thousands of brats are grilled and eaten with onions and mustard on the famous Wisconsin hard rolls, and washed down with foaming steins of locally brewed beer.

1½ lbs. pork butt	1 tsp. black pepper	
1 lb. veal shoulder	1 tsp. mace	
½ lb. pork back fat	1 tsp. ground caraway seed	
1 tbsp. salt	½ tsp. ground ginger	
1 tsp. sugar	½ cup milk	

Mix meat, fat, and seasonings in large bowl, and grind everything through ⅛-inch plate. Add milk, and knead until all is well mixed. Stuff into medium hog casings, and tie into 5-inch links.

Minnesota Potato Sausage

Pork skin adds texture and flavor to this delicious sausage. You can also use the rind from slab bacon or skin from a ham or pork shoulder.

⅓ lb. pork skin	1½ tbsp. kosher salt
1½ lbs. pork butt	2 tsp. dry mustard
1 lb. beef chuck	1 tsp. allspice
½ lb. pork back fat	2 tsp. fresh marjoram
2 lbs. boiling potatoes, peeled	2 tsp. caraway seed
2 medium onions	1½ tsp. black pepper

Cover pork skin with water, and bring to a boil. Cover pot and reduce heat to a simmer. Cook for 30 to 40 minutes until skin is soft. Cool under cold running water. Grind meats, fat, raw potatoes, onions, and pork skin through ¼-inch plate into large bowl. Add remaining ingredients, and knead until well blended. Moisten with a little water if needed to aid in mixing. Stuff into medium hog casings, and tie into 5- to 6-inch lengths. Poach in 180-degree water for 40 minutes. Remove and cool. This sausage will keep for 3 days refrigerated, 2 months frozen.

Lunenburg Sausage

10 lbs. ground pork	½ tsp. savory
7½ lbs. ground beef	1 tbsp. allspice
2 tbsp. salt	¼ cup coriander
2 oz. black pepper	

Mix all together. May be frozen in small amounts.

Iowa Farm Sausage

This basic American sage and pork sausage has a bit of garlic, fresh parsley, and just enough hot red pepper to give it a mild zing. Sausage like this is made all through the Midwest.

2¹/₄ lbs. pork butt	2 tsp. coarsely ground black pepper
³/₄ lbs. pork back fat	
2 tsp. sage	1 tsp. ground ginger
¹/₄ cup fine chopped parsley	¹/₂ tsp. minced garlic
1 tsp. thyme	¹/₄ cup chopped onion
1 tsp. basil	1 tbsp. kosher salt
1 tsp. red pepper flakes	¹/₄ cup water

Grind meat and fat together through ¹/₈- or ¹/₄-inch plate. Mix with all remaining ingredients, and knead until well blended. Package bulk sausage in plastic wrap. This fresh sausage will keep for 3 days refrigerated, 2 months frozen.

Missouri Dried Sausage

4 lbs. medium-ground beef chuck	4 tbsp. salt
	1 tbsp. black pepper
1 lb. fine-ground pork butt	1 cup brandy
4 tbsp. sugar	

Combine all ingredients, mix well, and refrigerate for 48 hours. Stuff into fiber or beef casings. Dry 5 to 9 weeks. Smoke with heavy cool smoke for 48 hours.

Kansas Country Sausage

10 lbs. fresh pork (¾ lean, ¼ fat)
 1 tbsp. black pepper
 2 tbsp. salt
 1 tsp. sage

Grind meat through fine blade of food or sausage mill. Mix well
with seasonings. Shape into small cakes or patties, and fry. Sausage
may be wrapped tightly and frozen, either before or after frying.

American Beef Sausage

 6 lbs. lean ground beef
 3 cups bread crumbs
 2 eggs, beaten
 3 tsp. salt
1½ tsp. freshly ground
      black pepper

 1 tsp. cayenne
 4 tbsp. fresh parsley,
      chopped
 2 tsp. sage
 1 cup water

Mix all ingredients thoroughly, and stuff into hog casings. Put
into boiling water to cover, and boil for ½ hour. Take from pot
and allow to cool, then refrigerate. Slice and broil to serve.

Southwestern Sausage Mixture

2¼ lbs. lean pork	1 tsp. freshly ground pepper
¾ lb. kidney suet	1½ tsp. cumin
½ cup finely chopped onion	1 tsp. coriander
5 cloves garlic, chopped	¼ cup brandy
4 to 6 chili peppers, chopped	½ cup vinegar
⅓ cup chili powder	½ tsp. Tabasco
salt	

Chop or grind pork coarsely, and combine with suet. Add remaining ingredients, and blend well. Stuff into casings, making 4-inch sausages. Hang in a dry place or in front of an electric fan for 24 hours. Store in refrigerator. Will keep for 2 weeks.

Rosemary Sausage

1½ lbs. fine-ground veal	1 tbsp. rosemary
2 lbs. fine-ground pork butt	1 tsp. thyme
1½ lbs. fine-ground beef chuck	1 tsp. nutmeg
1½ tbsp. salt	1 tsp. marjoram
2 tsp. black pepper	1 cup water

Combine all ingredients, and mix well. Stuff into hog casings. Bake, fry, or broil.

Chinese Pork and Shrimp Sausage

Pork and shrimp are often mixed as a stuffing for dim sum, the popular steamed dumplings served in the sometimes palatial teahouses of San Francisco's Chinatown. This sausage has a bit more flavor and spice than the typical dim sum filling and can be used in a variety of dishes.

2 lbs. pork shoulder
½ lb. shrimp, peeled and deveined
½ lb. pork back fat
4 tbsp. Chinese soy sauce
1 tsp. minced garlic

¼ cup finely chopped green onions or Chinese garlic chives
2 tsp. finely chopped fresh ginger
½ tsp. Chinese chili paste or 2 to 3 dashes Tabasco

Grind pork, shrimp, and fat through ¼-inch plate into large bowl. Add remaining ingredients, and knead mixture until well blended. Stuff into medium hog casings or leave in bulk for patties or meatballs. Keeps 3 days refrigerated, 2 months frozen.

Chinatown Crepinettes

3 lbs. pork shoulder	4 tsp. kosher salt
½ lb. pork back fat	1 tsp. black pepper
2 bunches cilantro or flat-leaf parsley, chopped fine	pinch of cinnamon
	2 tsp. Szechuan pepper- corns, roasted, ground
4 green onions, chopped fine	2 tsp. Chinese five spice or ground star anise
2 tsp. minced garlic	
¼ cup Chinese rice wine or Madeira	1 lb. caul fat, soaked (optional)

Grind meat and fat through ⅜-inch plate. Mix with all other ingredients except caul fat or casings, and blend thoroughly with your hands. Chill sausage meat for at least 1 hour or overnight. For crepinettes, spread out sheets of the lacy caul fat, and cut into 6-inch squares. Wrap each square around ⅓ cup meat mixture. Shape into ovals, and fry or grill over charcoal. To make links, stuff mixture into small sheep casings, and tie into 6-inch links.

Ginger Pork Sausage

5 lbs. medium-ground pork butt
5 tsp. salt
2 tsp. black pepper
2 tsp. ground ginger

Combine all ingredients, mix well, and stuff into hog casings. Pan fry.

Japantown Pork and Shiitake Mushroom Sausage

All along the West Coast and in Hawaii there are large Japanese-American communities, some going back decades, and the style, aesthetics, and seasonings of Japanese cooking are found in restaurants and home kitchens alike.

You can use this aromatic sausage in bulk to stuff wontons or pot stickers, called *gyoza* in Japanese kitchens. Or you can stuff the meat into casings for grilling.

2 lbs. pork shoulder	1 tsp. grated lime or
1/4 lb. pork back fat	lemon zest
3/4 lb. chicken thighs,	1 tsp. finely chopped
boned, with skin	ginger
12 oz. (4 to 6) dried shiitake	1 tsp. sugar
mushrooms	1 tbsp. sesame oil
4 tbsp. Japanese soy	2 tbsp. rice vinegar
sauce (shoyu)	
1/4 cup mirin, sake, or	
sweet sherry	

Soak mushrooms in hot water for 30 minutes. Remove and discard the tough stems; drain and chop mushrooms finely. Grind pork, chicken, and fat through 1/4-inch plate. Add all other ingredients, and mix well to blend. Stuff into medium hog casings or leave in bulk. Makes 3 1/2 pounds.

YUGOSLAVIA

Kranjska Kobascia
Kranj Sausages

12 lbs. cubed pork shoulder and rib trimmings	½ cup salt
2 lbs. cubed bacon	3 to 4½ tbsp. black pepper
1 clove garlic, crushed	3 tbsp. sodium nitrate
	1 cup water

Combine all ingredients, and knead for about 30 minutes. Fill into small sausage skins (hot casings), and tie together in pairs. Dry in smokehouse for 1 to 3 days; smoke longer if desired.

Krvave Klobase or Krvavice
Blood Sausage

3 large or 4 medium pork
heads (split, jaws removed,
thoroughly cleaned and
scoured) or 15 lbs. pork
shoulder meat
1 gallon or more pig blood
5½ lbs. long-grain rice
¼ cup rosemary

⅓ cup marjoram
¼ cup basil
2 tbsp. cinnamon
¾ cup salt
⅓ cup pepper
juice of 2 cloves garlic,
mashed and strained

Boil all meat to point where it falls off bone; reserve stock. Carefully clean meat of all bone, and put through fine grinder. Boil and cool rice. Combine all ingredients, adding blood last. (One gallon is usually enough, unless the meat mixture absorbs more; then add more, but not too much, as it will make the sausage dry.) Put mixture into sausage machine, and stuff pork casings, tying securely at desired length. Leave plenty of space for expansion during cooking. Boil sausage in reserved stock for about 12 minutes over medium heat. Carefully remove sausages with wooden spoon, and place side by side to cool on clean butcher paper spread over counter. When thoroughly cooled, wrap in freezer paper and freeze for future use. To serve, bake sausage for 45 minutes at 350 degrees. Frozen sausage may be placed directly into oven, but allow more baking time.

Klobase
Meat Sausage

70	lbs. pork shoulder	2½	cups salt
30	lbs. elk or deer meat (elk is preferable; pork may be substituted)	½	pkg. of FLB salt (may be omitted if not available) pepper
6	cloves garlic	11	cups water
1	cup sugar	3 to 4	cups wine (optional)

Dissolve both salts and sugar in 8 cups warm water. Mash garlic, and soak in 3 cups cold water for at least 2 hours. Then strain out and discard garlic, and add garlic water along with all other ingredients to ground meat in large tub or crock. The meat will absorb the water; more may be added during the mixing. Add wine for flavor and added moistness. After mixing thoroughly, grind, then stuff pork casings, twisting at desired length. Casings may be cut at desired lengths and ends skewered with toothpicks. Hang sausage overnight to dry, then hang in smokehouse. Smoke for at least 4 hours, or until desired color is obtained. Air sausage for at least 1 full day. It can be wrapped and put in freezer, canned, or better yet, just eaten. To serve, boil sausage for about 1 hour,

If canning, after sausage has been smoked, wipe with damp cloth and put into jars. Add hot water to jars. Put caps on, and boil in canner for 2 hours. To keep jars submerged, cover with board.

Pork and Liver Sausage with Slivovitz

These aromatic and flavorful sausages are delicious when cold smoked, but they also can be enjoyed fresh or air dried. They use slivovitz, the hot Yugoslavian plum brandy, as a flavoring, and its fruity aromas blend beautifully with the liver and spices. The mix of slivovitz, palinka, or other fruit brandies with spices, liver, and meat is typical of the peasant sausages made in Yugoslavia.

2 lbs. pork butt with some fat	½ tsp. ground ginger
	½ tsp. allspice
1 lb. pork or beef liver	¼ tsp. nutmeg
1 cup finely chopped onions	1 tsp. thyme
1 tbsp. oil	¼ cup slivovitz or kirsch
4 tsp. kosher salt	½ cup water
2 tsp. black pepper	1 tsp. curing salt (optional)

Poach liver until firm, about 5 minutes. Cook onions, covered, in oil for 5 minutes, or until translucent. Grind pork, liver, and onions through fine, ⅛-inch plate. Add remaining ingredients, and moisten with enough water to blend everything well. Stuff into medium hog casings, and tie into 7-inch links. Air-dry overnight in a cool place and cold smoke for at least 8 hours, or use sausages fresh. Use curing salts if you air-dry or cold smoke sausages.

Part 3
Specialty Recipes

Seafood Sausages

Seafood as an ingredient for sausage never has and probably never will be very popular, although a very tasty sausage can be made from the bounty of the sea.

There is no reason why a regular sausage seasoning cannot be used for seafood sausages; however, dill is sometimes added to seafood recipes.

Atlantic Seafood Sausage

The ingredients that inspired these fish sausages are part of the bounty of the North Atlantic: cod, clams, scallops, and lobster. Any firm, white-fleshed fish can be used here instead of cod, and shrimp can replace the lobster.

1½ lbs. cod fillets
¼ lb. diced cooked clams
¼ lb. small bay scallops cut in half, or diced sea scallops
1 cup diced cooked lobster
2 egg whites
1½ cups heavy cream

2 tsp. kosher salt
½ tsp. finely ground black pepper
1 tsp. fresh chopped or ½ tsp. dried thyme
2 tsp. tomato paste
3 tbsp. sweet sherry

Put food processor bowl and metal blade into freezer for at least 30 minutes before starting. Cut cod into ¾-inch chunks, and freeze for 15 minutes. Then, using metal blade, process cod until smooth. With motor running, gradually add egg whites until they are fully incorporated. Pour in cream in a steady stream until it is thoroughly blended. Add salt, pepper, tomato paste, and thyme, and process 10 seconds. Transfer fish mixture to bowl, and fold in remaining ingredients, until everything is well blended. Make a small ball of the mixture, poach in simmering water for 5 minutes, and check for proper seasoning. Stuff into sheep casings, and tie into 6-inch links.

Bring large pot of lightly salted water to a boil. Put in sausages, and adjust heat to below simmer, about 180 degrees. Poach sausages for about 15 minutes, or until firm. Drain and serve immediately, or cool under running water and refrigerate. Makes about 2½ pounds.

Seaman's Sausage

2 lbs. fish	¼ tsp. cayenne pepper
1 medium onion	20 single saltine crackers
freshly ground	½ tsp. salt
black pepper	1 tsp. poultry seasoning
¼ tsp. celery salt	¼ tsp. garlic powder
2 tsp. Dijon mustard	1 tbsp. lemon juice

Use boneless, skinless fish scraps or fillets. Use steel blade of food processor, and process finely ground, in ½-pound batches. Toss in peeled and chopped onion and crackers, and give them a good blast on the button. Mix with fish into large bowl, add remaining ingredients, and blend with your hands until thoroughly combined. Form into 12 patties, and fry in butter or bacon fat over medium heat until brown on both sides.

Oyster Sausage

1 lb. veal	1 slice bread
20 oysters	1 egg
small amount of suet	black pepper

Pound veal very finely in mortar with a little suet; season with pepper. Cut oysters into pieces. Soak bread in oyster liquid, pound it, and mix with oysters and veal. Beat egg and add as a binder; mix well. Roll mixture into little links, like sausages. Fry in pan, turning frequently, and serve.

Razor Clam Sausage

---

4 lbs. razor clams, chopped
2 eggs, slightly beaten
4 large onions, diced
  bread crumbs

sage
ground cloves
liquid garlic
dill salt

Combine all ingredients, and form into patties, fry and serve.

Note: Clam-based sausage is very good made into patties, but when stuffed into casings there is too much moisture and they tend to burst when frying.

Fish Sausage

---

5 lbs. fish fillets
4 white rolls
2 cups milk
8 eggs

4 tbsp. parsley
1 tsp. pepper
2 tsp. salt

Soak rolls in milk, squeeze, shred, and mix with all other ingredients. Stuff into sheep casings and fry or broil until browned, turning frequently.

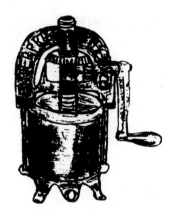

Wild Game
Sausages

I would be repetitious if I gave you a full course in game sausage, because most game can be substituted for beef in any recipe in this book, with some adjustments made for fat content. The fat of most game animals is the most important factor as to whether your game sausage is palatable. Do not use any of the fat from venison, bear, or antelope in sausage; instead, use beef suet or pork fat. Moose or elk fat may be used, however.

How much fat do you need to use? The beef called for in a recipe has a percentage of fat, so if substituting a game meat from which all the fat has been removed, add beef suet or pork fat in an amount equivalent to the fat removed.

Also keep in mind that good sausage cannot be made from poor-quality products; therefore, do not use the trimmings from the bullet hole region. Even more important, be sure that the animal is adequately dressed and taken care of when killed. Deterioration begins very quickly, especially with a heavy-skinned animal such as an elk or moose, and more so if the weather is warm.

Many people out hunting big game have suddenly been startled and pleased to find themselves standing over the carcass of an animal just shot. Now what do you do? There is an abundance of books and articles on taking care of your game in the field; if you do not know what to do, obtain such a reference and follow the instructions. Palatable food is nearly always dependent on proper harvesting, storage, transportation, and preparation. If you want to ruin the meat, just put it on the fender and drive home many miles.

When you get your animal home, let the heat out by removing the skin—the animal's natural insulation—and quickly get the meat under refrigeration at 40 degrees or less. The animal may be cut up and put into an extra refrigerator. Be sure there is air space between the cuts of quarters of meat placed in the refrigerator.

The tougher parts of your animal and the trimmings that usually end up as hamburger will make very good sausage if proper procedures are followed. When making sausage from game I have bagged, I make a few half-size links in either natural or cloth casings so that I can give my friends each a full sausage, rather than half of a larger one.

The hardest part of any wild game sausage recipe is getting the game. I never buy my casings before I go hunting!

Game Sausage

This recipe will work for deer, reindeer, caribou, or moose.

10 lbs. clean, fresh game from trimmings and tough cuts	6 tbsp. salt
10 lbs. pork	2 tbsp. pepper
	pinch of sage

Grind meats and seasonings together thoroughly. Stuff into casings, and smoke for 8 to 10 hours at 110 degrees.

Venison Sausage #1

6 lbs. lean venison
6 lbs. pork, not too lean
1 tbsp. garlic powder
1/4 cup salt
1 1/2 tbsp. black pepper

1 tbsp. saltpeter
1/4 tsp. allspice
1 tbsp. crushed chili
 pepper (optional)

Cut venison and pork into small chunks for grinder. Add seasonings, mix thoroughly, and put through grinder, using medium blade. Use as any fresh sausage: Store in freezer or stuff in pork or sheep casings, then give a long smoking at a low temperature to enhance the flavor.

Venison Sausage #2

30 lbs. chopped venison
10 lbs. chopped fat (50% lean)
1 lb. salt

3 oz. black pepper
2 oz. sage
1 oz. red pepper

Mix together venison and fat pork. Add seasonings, and mix thoroughly. Put through coarse plate of grinder, then fine plate. This can be stuffed into casings or made into patties for frying.

Venison Sausage #3

10 lbs. clean venison,
   trimmed of fat
10 lbs. pork butt
6 tbsp. salt

2 tbsp. black pepper
1/2 tsp. sage
1/4 tsp. garlic powder

Cut venison and pork into 1-inch cubes. Mix meats together, and spread on large cookie sheet. Mix seasonings together, and sprinkle over meat mixture. Let mixture stand for 2 hours in a cool place, then grind. Mix thoroughly with your hands, distributing the seasonings thoroughly. Then stuff into hog casings, and make rings about the size of ring bologna. Smoke for 8 to 10 hours at 110 degrees.

Venison Sausage #4

5 lbs. venison, trimmed of fat
1 lb. fresh side pork
1 lb. salt pork
4 tsp. powdered sage
5 tsp. salt

3 tsp. black pepper
2 tsp. cayenne
1/8 tsp. garlic powder
1/2 lemon rind, grated

Cut meats into 1-inch cubes, mix together, and spread out on large pan. Mix seasonings, and sprinkle over meat mixture. Grind using 3/16-inch plate. Mix ground meats, then stuff into hog casings, making rings or links any size you desire. Use fresh or smoke 6 to 8 hours at 110 degrees. If frozen, use within 3 months.

Venison Sausage Links: Mild

5 lbs. chopped venison	2 tbsp. salt
1 lb. beef suet, pork fat, or bacon, in cubes	1 tbsp. black pepper
1/4 cup honey	1/2 tsp. red or cayenne pepper
red wine (optional)	1/2 tsp. saltpeter
1 tbsp. monosodium glutamate (optional)	

Put venison and fat in suitable pan. Spread all other ingredients over meat, and mix thoroughly. Put through coarse grinder plate, then fine plate. Be sure to keep meat cold, or mix in some ice cubes. Water is often necessary to make a suitable stuffing consistency. Stuff into sheep casings, and make links. May be cold smoked if desired.

Venison Sausage Links: Hot

5 lbs. chopped venison	2 tbsp. freshly ground black pepper
1 lb. beef suet, pork fat, or bacon, in cubes	1 tsp. red or cayenne pepper
red wine (optional)	1 tsp. sage
1 tbsp. monosodium glutamate (optional)	1 tsp. paprika
2 tbsp. salt	

Follow procedure for Venison Sausage Links: Mild.

Bulk Venison Sausage #1

3 lbs. chopped venison
1 lb. beef suet, pork fat, or bacon, in cubes
4 tbsp. sausage seasoning

Grind venison through coarse cutter plate, spread out in pan, and sprinkle seasoning over it evenly. Grind fat into smaller pieces than venison, add to venison mixture, and mix together. Let sausage sit in refrigerator for 1 or 2 days, then freeze any that you won't be eating within a few days.

Bulk Venison Sausage #2

5 lbs. chopped venison
1 lb. beef suet, pork fat,
   or bacon, in cubes
2 tbsp. salt
2 tsp. black pepper
1 tsp. red or cayenne
   pepper

1 tbsp. monosodium
   glutamate
3 tbsp. sage
$\frac{1}{2}$ tsp. saltpeter
2 tbsp. molasses
$\frac{1}{2}$ cup water

Grind meat and fat following directions for Bulk Venison Sausage #1, mixing dry seasonings and saltpeter together and sprinkling evenly over meat. Then grind meat and fat together through medium plate, and put in large container. Mix molasses with water, add to meat, and mix well. Store for a day, then cut and freeze.

Venison Potato Sausage

4 lbs. venison	3½ lbs. potatoes
1 lb. beef	2 tbsp. salt
2 lbs. lean pork	1 tsp. pepper
1 large onion	1 tsp. allspice

Grind meats and onion. Wash, peel, and grind potatoes. Combine all ingredients, and mix thoroughly. Fill into casings, using sausage stuffer; do not stuff casings too full. After stuffing, tie ends of sausages with string. Submerge in large kettle of cold water, and bring to a boil. Boil about 1 hour at 325 degrees. Prick each sausage with fork after first 10 minutes of boiling. Serve hot or cold, or store in a cold place for later use. Flavor is at its best when sausage is fried in skillet until casings are golden brown.

Venison Sausage Patties

2½ lbs. venison, trimmed of fat	2 tsp. black pepper
2 lbs. pork butt	¼ tsp. sage
½ lb. fresh side pork	¼ tsp. cayenne
5 tsp. salt	

Using ⅜-inch plate, grind meats. Alternate venison and pork as you grind. Spread ground meat on cookie sheet. Blend seasonings, and work into meat. Then grind again using ³⁄₁₆-inch plate. Work mixture well with your hands to distribute seasonings. Shape into patties, pack into plastic bags, and freeze. You may also shape into rolls for slicing and keep in refrigerator for a short time. Either way, use within 1 month.

Wyoming Polish Sausage

17 lbs. lean venison
17 lbs. lean pork
 2 tsp. garlic powder or
    onion powder
1½ oz. nutmeg

½ oz. paprika
½ oz. salt
½ lb. dried milk
½ oz. allspice

Cube meat, sprinkle with spices, and mix with other ingredients. Grind meats using medium blade. Add water or ice cubes before grinding if meat is too warm. Stuff into hog or muslin casings, or make into patties. Sausage in casings may be cold smoked if desired.

Cured Game Sausage

This recipe is good with elk, venison, or moose.

1 lb. meat from game
1 lb. fat pork
1 tsp. black pepper
3 lbs. dry cure mix

½ tsp. ground cloves
1 tsp. sage
  red wine (optional)

Cut or cube meats suitable for grinder, add seasonings, mix thoroughly, and put through grinder. For medium-coarse texture, put twice through ⅜-inch plate. For fine texture, put once through ⅜-inch plate and once through ⅛-inch plate. Place meat in shallow container, and keep under refrigeration at about 40 degrees for 3 to 4 days. Add wine as a marinade, if desired, and let sit another day. Stuff into casings. Cool smoke if desired.

Smoked Venison Country Sausage

30 lbs. venison	8 oz. sugar
20 lbs. pork or beef (50% fat)	4 oz. onion powder
14 cups water	2 oz. paprika
1½ lbs. salt	2 oz. cure
2 oz. white pepper	1 oz. nutmeg
2 oz. monosodium glutamate	1 oz. allspice

Grind meats through fine plate. Mix remaining ingredients for about 5 minutes. Stuff into hog casings. Smoke for 3 hours at 190 degrees. Cook in water at 160 degrees until temperature of sausage reaches 150 degrees. Store in refrigerator.

Venison Thuringer

30 lbs. venison	½ lb. sugar
20 lbs. beef (50% fat)	1½ oz. paprika
7½ lbs. water	1 oz. coriander
1¼ lbs. salt	1 oz. nutmeg
2½ oz. white pepper	1½ oz. dry mustard
1½ oz. liquid smoke	1½ oz. cure
7/16 oz. sodium erythorbate	

Grind meats through fine plate. Add remaining ingredients, and mix for 6 minutes. Stuff into casings. Cook in smokehouse at 170 degrees until internal temperature of sausages is 150 degrees. Cool in water until internal temperature is below 90 degrees. Store in refrigerator.

Venison Polish Sausage

25	lbs. venison	7/16	oz. sodium erythorbate
25	lbs. pork	6	oz. sugar
12	cups water	2	oz. garlic powder
1¼	lbs. salt	1	oz. nutmeg
2½	oz. white pepper	¾	oz. ground celery seed
1	oz. monosodium	¾	oz. coriander
	glutamate	1½	oz. cure

Grind pork and half of venison through medium plate. Grind other half of venison through fine plate. Mix together with all other ingredients for 5 minutes. Stuff into hog casings. Smoke for 2½ hours at 190 degrees for desired color. Cook in water at 160 degrees until internal temperature of the sausage reaches 150 degrees. Cool in water until internal temperature is below 90 degrees. Store in refrigerator.

Venison Summer Sausage

35	lbs. venison	12	cups water
15	lbs. beef trimmings (50% fat)	½	lb. sugar
1½	lb. nonfat dry milk	1½	lbs. salt
6	oz. mustard seed	1½	oz. cure
7/16	oz. sodium erythorbate	2½	oz. liquid smoke
3	oz. white pepper		

Grind through fine plate. Combine all ingredients, and mix for about 6 minutes. Stuff into artificial casings. Cook in smokehouse at 190 degrees until internal temperature of sausages is 150 degrees. Cool in water until internal temperature is below 90 degrees. Store in refrigerator.

Hunter's Delight Venison Sausage

4 lbs. venison or beef, cut
   into 1½-inch cubes
4 lbs. pork butt or pork
   shoulder, cut into
   1½-inch cubes
2 tbsp. salt
2 tsp. coarsely ground
   black pepper

¾ tsp. mace
¼ tsp. ground cloves
¼ tsp. nutmeg
½ tsp. allspice
½ tsp. garlic powder

Cut meats into 1½-inch cubes. Combine seasonings, and sprinkle
over meat, in large bowl. Toss until well coated. Grind with desired
plate, and stuff into casings. Smoke for 8 to 10 hours.

Specialty Sausages

Specialty sausages use a variety of different cuts of meat. Some types of specialty sausages are very familiar, some are less so.

BOLOGNA

Bologna was invented in the town of Bologna, Italy, in 1463 by a man named Anthony Garcia. Bologna grew in popularity, and bologna making spread rapidly to nearly every country in the world. It is one of our most commonly used sausages today.

Bologna sausage consists of ground pork and beef mixed with enough water to give the sausage the desirable fine texture. For mild, fine-tasting bologna, cook it using the Garcia method: using a fork, jab holes into the ring of bologna about $1/4$ inch apart on both sides. Then prepare as usual. Piercing the casing prevents strong-tasting, greasy bologna. Bologna cooked in this fashion is one of the world's really great delicacies.

Bologna

25 lbs. beef	1/4 oz., saltpeter dissolved
5 lbs. pork	in warm water
2 1/2 cups salt	1/2 oz. cloves
2 1/2 oz. black pepper	2 lbs. brown sugar
	3/4 oz. mace

Combine all ingredients, mix well, and grind. Make bags from new muslin. With seams on outside, fill with bologna mixture. Smoke as desired.

American Bologna

15 lbs. beef, cured	1 1/4 oz. white pepper
5 lbs. fat pork, cured	1/4 oz. coriander
5 lbs. cook pork tripe	1/4 oz. ground ginger
1 lb. farina	1/4 oz. dry mustard
10 cups ice water	1/4 oz. ground nutmeg

Break down meats, and place in bowl chopper. Add remaining ingredients, and mix well. Stuff into bungs or synthetic casings, and tie with string at about 3-inch intervals. Smoke for about 3 hours, starting at 110 degrees, and increasing to 150 degrees just before removal. Then immerse in water at 160 to 170 degrees for 2 1/2 to 3 hours, depending on size. Chill in cold water for 15 minutes or use a cold spray. Shrinkage may be about 10 percent.

Bologna Sausage

2 lbs. lean pork	1 oz. mixed parsley,
2 lbs. lean veal	savory, marjoram,
2 lbs. fresh lean beef	and thyme
2 lbs. fat salt pork	2 tsp. cayenne
1 lb. beef suet	2 tsp. black pepper
1 onion, minced	1 nutmeg, grated
salt	1 tsp. cloves
10 tsp. sage	oil or melted butter

Chop or grind meats and suet. Add onion and seasonings, and mix well. Stuff into beef skins, and tie them up. Prick each in several places to allow steam to escape. Put into hot water, and heat gradually to boiling. Cook slowly for 1 hour. Remove and lay sausages on clean straw or hay in sun to dry. Rub outside of skins with oil or melted butter, and place in cool, dry cellar. If you want to keep them more than 1 week, rub with ginger or pepper; wash off before using. No further cooking is needed.

Country-Style Bologna

40 lbs. lean beef chuck	1 oz. sodium nitrate
10 lbs. regular pork trimmings	1/8 oz. sodium nitrite
5 lbs. shaved ice or water	1 oz. coriander
1 1/2 lbs. salt	3 oz. white pepper
4 oz. sugar	

Grind meats through 1/4-inch plate, add seasonings, mix well, and regrind. Stuff into small casings in 15-inch lengths, and tie ends together. When dry, smoke in smokehouse to desired color, then cook at 170 degrees until inside temperature of bologna reaches 155 degrees.

Old-Recipe Bologna

37½ lbs. ground beef
2½ lbs. brown sugar
2 lbs. salt
1½ oz. pepper
1 oz. saltpeter

Combine all ingredients, mix well, and stuff into muslin sacks 4 inches wide and 24 to 30 inches long. Hang in cellar for 1 week, then smoke to improve flavor. Keep in a dry place 6 to 8 weeks before using.

A coat of paraffin applied to bags with a brush will help to preserve bologna.

Cured Bologna

3 lbs. beef
2 lbs. lean pork
⅔ cup dry cure mix

2½ tsp. black pepper
½ tsp. coriander
½ tsp. mace

Coarse-grind chopped beef with 2½ tablespoons dry cure. Cut pork into small pieces, mix with 1½ tablespoons dry cure, and coarse-grind. Put ground meats, separately, in a cold place to cure for 48 hours. Then mix meats together, add seasonings, and mix all together well. Run through fine grinder and stuff into large muslin casings. Hang in a cool place for 8 hours. Smoke for 4 hours at 100 degrees, using plenty of smoke. Place in hot water, and simmer until they float. Cool quickly in ice-cold water, and hang to dry in a cool place.

Farmhouse Bologna Sausage

6 lbs. beef trimmings	2 tsp. coriander
4 lbs. pork trimmings	½ tsp. mace
3 or 5 tbsp. salt	¼ oz. saltpeter
1 tbsp. black pepper	1 qt. cold water

If pork trimmings are fresh, use 5 tablespoons salt; if pork is cured, use 3 tablespoons.

Grind chilled beef trimmings with 3 tablespoons salt, using coarse grinder plate. Put in bowl, cover with waxed paper, and refrigerate for 48 hours.

On second day, grind pork using coarse plate. Put in bowl, cover with waxed paper, and refrigerate 24 hours.

On third day, regrind beef using fine grinder. Add pork and, if necessary, additional 2 tablespoons salt. Grind meats together using fine plate. Add water and seasonings, and mix well, until mixture becomes a sticky mass. Stuff tightly into beef casings. Hang in a cool place overnight, then smoke for 2 hours in well-ventilated smokehouse that has been heated to 110 to 120 degrees.

Put hot, smoked sausage in water heated to 160 to 175 degrees, and let simmer 15 to 30 minutes, until sausage squeaks when pressed and released. Plunge into cold water to chill, and hang to drip dry. Refrigerate until used. May be frozen.

Weasand Bologna

30 lbs. beef trimmings	½ tbsp. Zanzibar garlic
15 lbs. pork trimmings	compound
5 lbs. back or jowl fat	Bull Meat brand flour
½ lb. Zanzibar bologna	cracked ice or water
sausage seasoning	

All meats should first be cured with Freeze-Em-Pickle. Chop beef trimmings very fine in silent cutter, adding dry ingredients while cutting. When thoroughly mixed, add pork trimmings and allow machine to make four turns. Then add back or jowl fat, gradually adding ice or ice water to cool meat while grinding and give proper consistency. Chop until fat pieces are about size of peas. Remove meat from machine and immediately stuff into No. 1 beef weasands, puncturing thoroughly to let air out. Close open end with skewer, and tie with 3-inch loops for smoke stick. Smoke sufficiently, then remove from smokehouse and cook in water 155 to 160 degrees for 40 to 60 minutes, according to thickness of sausage. Hang at room temperature until dry on surface and cooled through, then move to cooler.

KOSHER SAUSAGES

"And the swine . . . shall be unclean to you."

Moses' law against eating pork, echoed by Mohammed and followed by the Yakuts of Turkey, the Laplanders, natives of Borneo, Indians of the Guianas, and America's Navajos, few of whom ever heard of Moses, is often hailed as the oldest law of hygiene and evidence of the antiquity of trichinosis. Few anthropologists, however, think the Mosaic law had anything to do with hygiene. Symptoms of trichinosis develop so long after infection that the significance of uncooked pork as a source of the disease was discovered only comparatively recently.

The sausages in this section contain no pork or pork products.

Tiny Sausages

These are a favorite for Passover parties.

1 lb. chopped beef	1 egg
salt (optional)	2 tbsp. cold water
1 onion, grated	fine matzo meal
1 small carrot	

Combine meat, onion, egg beaten with water, and salt if desired. Grate in carrot, and mix well. Form ½-inch-thick sausage links about 2½ inches long. Roll in matzo meal, and fry until browned on all sides. Drain excess fat on paper towel. Makes about 24 sausages.

Kosher Salami

20	lbs. lean bull beef	$\frac{1}{2}$ oz. nutmeg	
7$\frac{1}{2}$	lbs. brisket fat	$\frac{1}{2}$ oz. cardamom	
3$\frac{1}{2}$	oz. white pepper	$\frac{1}{4}$ oz. whole peppercorns	
1$\frac{1}{2}$	oz. coriander	$\frac{1}{4}$ oz. garlic powder	

Cure meat in small cubes. Grind through ⅜-inch plate, followed by fine plate. Add seasonings to meat, and mix well. Fill into kosher weasands, and hang for 24 hours. Then smoke, starting at 130 degrees and raising temperature to 160 degrees. Hold at 160 degrees for about 2 hours, until inside temperature of sausage is 140 degrees. Then chill in cold water or spray for 15 minutes.

Cellulose casings also may be used for kosher products, as no animal product is used in their manufacture. If desired, the Rabbinical Seal can be obtained on such casings.

Kosher Bologna

35 lbs. beef chuck trimmings, cured	$\frac{1}{16}$ lb. coriander
	$\frac{1}{16}$ lb. ginger
15 lbs. beef trimmings (briskets, plates, etc.)	$\frac{1}{16}$ lb. nutmeg
	$\frac{1}{2}$ oz. garlic compound
$\frac{1}{2}$ lb. bologna sausage seasoning	$\frac{1}{4}$ lb. sugar
	Bull Meat brand flour
	ice or ice water

Put beef into silent cutter, and chop fine or run through $\frac{5}{16}$-inch plate of meat grinder. While grinding, gradually add crushed ice or ice water. When cut fine, add remaining ingredients, including enough flour to reach desired consistency, and mix well. Stuff into beef rounds to make round bologna, beef middles to make long bologna, or beef bungs to make large bologna. Smoke bologna in smokehouse.

After sausage is smoked, cook as follows: round bologna for 30 minutes in water held at 160 degrees; long bologna for 40 to 60 minutes, according to thickness, at 160 degrees; and large bologna for $1\frac{1}{4}$ to 3 hours, according to thickness, at 155 degrees. When cooked, hang up and rinse with boiling water and then with cold water for a few minutes. Then hang at room temperature for a few hours to cool before refrigerating.

Kosher Beef Sausage

25 lbs. beef trimmings, cured	¼ lb. sugar
12½ lbs. beef plate trimmings, cured	½ oz. garlic compound flour
12½ lbs. brisket, cured	ice or ice water
½ lb. frankfurt sausage seasoning	

Put beef trimmings and plate beef through ⁵/₆₄-inch plate of grinder, and brisket through ¼-inch plate. Add sufficient ice or ice water while grinding. Put all meats into mixer or mix by hand in tub, and add remaining ingredients, including enough flour to reach desired consistency. When well mixed, stuff into beef round casings, and link into 1-pound rings. Hang in smokehouse, and give medium-hot smoke. Let cool, then hang in refrigerator. To serve, cook at 160 degrees for 30 minutes; serve hot.

Kosher Garlic Sausage

43½ lbs. beef trimmings, cured	¼ lb. sugar
7½ lbs. beef brisket fat, cured	1 oz. garlic compound
½ lb. bologna sausage seasoning	ice or ice water
	flour

Rub beef trimmings through ⁵⁄₆₄-inch plate of grinder, gradually adding ice or ice water while grinding. Grind brisket fat through ³⁄₁₆-inch plate. Combine in mixer with remaining ingredients, including enough flour to reach desired consistency, and mix for 5 minutes. Stuff into beef round casings, about 1 pound to the ring. Make one twist in center at bottom of each sausage, thus forming two links. Then tie ends together, leaving a 1-inch loop of twine between them. Sausage may also be made into ring form without linking. Smoke for 2 to 3 hours, then cook for 30 minutes in 155-degree water. If a bright color is desired, dip in a casing-brown mixture. After cooking, rinse sausage first with boiling water, then with cold. Allow to cool for 1 hour, then refrigerate.

Kosher Bratwurst

---

20 lbs. beef chuck trimmings
30 lbs. veal flank, briskets,
    or trimmings
$\frac{1}{2}$ lb. frankfurt sausage
    seasoning
$\frac{1}{8}$ lb. ground allspice

$\frac{1}{8}$ lb. dried marjoram
    cracked ice or ice water
$\frac{1}{4}$ lb. sugar
$\frac{1}{2}$ oz. garlic compound
    flour
1 lb. salt

Trim meats thoroughly, removing all skin, sinews, blood clot, and bones, but leaving the fat. Put beef through $\frac{5}{16}$-inch plate of grinder, and veal through $\frac{1}{8}$-inch plate. Put meats into mixer and mix, gradually adding ice or ice water and enough flour to reach desired consistency. Then mix in remaining ingredients. Stuff into narrow beef round casings or wide sheep casings, and tie with twine into links about 4 inches long. Cut in lengths of four links each, and hang on sticks, two links on each side. Cook for about 10 minutes at 155 to 160 degrees before eating.

Kosher Frankfurters
or Vienna Sausages

To make kosher frankfurters or Vienna sausages, follow procedure for Kosher Bratwurst, increasing garlic compound to 1 ounce. Then smoke at medium heat until they are a bright reddish brown, and cook for about 10 minutes at 155 to 160 degrees.

Kosher Liver Sausage

20 lbs. cooked calf head meat or beef cheek meat	1 lb. onions, finely chopped
7½ lbs. beef or calf hearts	1 lb. salt
15 lbs. beef or calf liver, scalded and soaked	½ lb. liver sausage seasoning
7½ lbs. beef tripe	Bull Meat brand flour
	cracked ice or ice water

Run meat and hearts through ⁵⁄₆₄-inch plate. Work a little ice water into it while grinding, then put into mixer or hand mix in tub. If meat is chopped in silent cutter instead of grinding, ice water should slowly be added while chopping, as no mixing is needed afterward. Add enough flour to reach desired consistency. Grind liver through ⁵⁄₆₄-inch plate, and add to ground or chopped meat in mixer. Run tripe through finest plate of meat grinder and add to meat and liver. Add remaining ingredients, and mix well, adding more ice or ice water until mixture is soft and pasty. Stuff into beef middles, and cook for 30 to 40 minutes at 150 to 155 degrees. Then chill sausage well in cold water, dry by hanging at room temperature, and place in cooler.

Kosher Liver Sausage with Veal

12½ lbs. calf liver, scalded and soaked	1 salt
5 lbs. brisket fat	½ lb. liver sausage seasoning
32½ lbs. veal	Bull Meat brand flour
1 lb. onions, finely chopped	cracked ice or ice water

Follow procedure for Kosher Liver Sausage, ignoring instructions for hearts and tripe but cutting brisket fat into small cubes or running it through ¼-inch hole and adding to meat and liver.

Kosher Cervalet or Summer Sausage

37½ lbs. lean beef trimmings	½ lb. Freeze-Em-Pickle
12½ lbs. fat beef brisket	¼ lb. sugar
¾ lbs. salt	flour
½ lbs. summer or cervalet sausage seasoning	

Chop beef trimmings medium fine and beef brisket coarse. While chopping, add other ingredients. Pack chopped meat tightly, not over 6 to 8 inches deep, into shallow pans or boxes. Cure in cooler at 38 to 40 degrees for 4 to 6 days. Then stuff into fully cured beef middles. Hang in a dry room at 48 to 56 degrees for 1 to 3 weeks. When dry, cold smoke.

Kosher Mettwurst

40 lbs. beef chuck trimmings, cured	1 tbsp. garlic compound
10 lbs. briskets, cured	$\frac{1}{4}$ lb. sugar
$\frac{1}{2}$ lb. mettwurst seasoning	flour
	$\frac{1}{2}$ lb. Freeze-Em-Pickle

Trim meats well, leaving all the fat on but removing gristle, skin, and bone, and cut into walnut-size pieces. Cure meat for about 1 week with Freeze-Em-Pickle cure. When cured, run through $\frac{1}{8}$-inch plate, and place in mixer or mix by hand. Add remaining ingredients, and mix well. Stuff tightly into beef round casings, in about 1-pound rings. Tie ends together, leaving loop of twine between the two ends for hanging purposes. Smoke for 24 to 36 hours in a slow, cold smoke. Allow to set. Sausage is ready to eat.

Dried Kosher Mettwurst

Follow procedure for Kosher Mettwurst, but stuff mixture into beef middles or weasands, and twine as done for salami sausage. Smoke in cold water for 24 to 36 hours, and then place in a dry room at 48 to 56 degrees.

HOT DOGS

Also known as frankfurters, hot dogs trace their origins back to Europe, but they are a part of American tradition.

According to some historians, the first wiener was served at the Saint Louis Exposition in 1904 by a Bavarian sausage peddler. He called his sausages "red hots." Since the "red hots" were too hot to handle, he provided his customers with pairs of white gloves. But gloves were expensive, so he came up with the idea of making a bun to fit the sausage.

About the same time, Harry Stevens, owner of a refreshment stand at the New York Polo Grounds, was searching for hot food for chilled football fans. He decided on sausages. His salesmen wandered through the stands shouting, "They're red hot. Get your red hot dachshund sausages."

Ted Dorgan, a sports humorist and cartoonist, was a spectator that day. Inspired by the "red hot dachshund sausages," he developed a cartoon on the theme. Hurrying to meet his deadline, Dorgan realized he couldn't spell "dachshund," so he settled for "dog." Thus was born the all-American hot dog.

Whether it is called hot dog, wiener, coney, frankfurter, or frank, this versatile meat is the most popular type of sausage in the United States. Hot dogs are made with beef, pork, and sometimes veal, combined with spices and seasonings. Today they also come in chicken and turkey varieties. The meat is stuffed into tender casings and smoked. This nutritious sausage is not only delicious, but high in protein too. One hot dog contains about 5.6 grams of protein—as much as a medium-size egg.

Americans do love hot dogs: They consume more than 2 billion pounds per year!

American-Style Frankfurter

16 lbs. pork	2 lbs. farina
8 lbs. bull meat	3 oz. white pepper
8 lbs. ox cheek	½ oz. ground ginger
8 lbs. veal	½ oz. coriander
6 lbs. tripe, cooked	½ oz. mace
18 cups ice water	

Dry-cure meats, then break down on mincer and transfer to bowl chopper in the following order: cheek meat, bull beef, then veal. Chop for a short period, then add cereal, seasonings, water, pork, and tripe. Continue chopping until all water is taken up. Fill into sheep or narrow hog casings, and link. Allow to dry, then smoke until desired color is obtained. Cook at 160 to 170 degrees for about 10 minutes. Spray with cold water to prevent shrinking and maintain the plump appearance. Store at about 45 degrees.

Milwaukee Frankfurter

20 lbs. pork trimmings
    (60% lean)
17½ lbs. regular pork trimmings
5 lbs. beef trimmings
5 lbs. lean veal
2½ lbs. pork neck bone
    trimmings
15 lbs. ice
1 lb., 4 oz salt

8 oz. corn syrup
4 oz. sugar
2 oz. white pepper
1 oz. monosodium
    glutamate
½ oz. nutmeg
½ oz. ginger
¼ oz. sodium nitrite

Chop beef, veal, and neck bone trimmings with ice, salt, and sodium nitrite to a smooth paste. Grind pork trimmings through ¼-inch plate. Mix all together with spices in mixer for 5 to 6 minutes. Transfer to stuffer, and stuff into size 25 cellulose casings. Link at 4-inch intervals. Heat in smokehouse at 120 degrees for 30 minutes, raise temperature to 140 degrees for 30 minutes, and then to 160 to 165 degrees, until an internal temperature of 152 degrees is reached. Cold shower for 5 minutes. Allow surface to dry, and place frankfurters in cooler at 34 to 38 degrees, then package.

Vienna Sausages

20	lbs. beef	3	oz. black pepper
10	lbs. fat pork	½ to ¾	lb. salt
1½	oz. sage, mace,	8	cups water
	or nutmeg		
	garlic or onions		
	(optional)		

Cut meats into same-size pieces. Mix seasonings, garlic, and onion together, then mix well with meats and put through fine plate of grinder. Grind two or three times to make sure seasonings are evenly distributed and meat is ground very fine. Add water, and mix thoroughly to make a pliable mass. Stuff into sheep or hog casings, depending on whether you want fat or thin frankfurters. After sausage is stuffed into casings, press casings together with thumb and forefinger at about 4-inch intervals. Twist first link two or three times; twist the next link in the opposite direction to keep casing from untwisting, and so on. Hang twisted links in smokehouse, and smoke at a temperature not over 125 degrees for about 2 hours, until they are a rich orange color. Then cook in 155-degree water until they float. If water is hotter, casings may burst. Required cooking time depends on thickness of frankfurters. After cooking, rinse in hot water, plunge into cold water, and hang in a cool place. Frankfurters should be used soon after they are made. If you wish to keep them longer, they should be canned.

White-Hot Frankfurter

25 lbs. regular pork trimmings	6 lbs. cracker meal
12½ lbs. lean veal	2 lbs. salt
12½ lbs. whole carcass beef	1 lb. corn syrup
30 lbs. ice or ice water	3 oz. white pepper

Grind beef and veal through ⅛-inch plate and pork through ¼-inch plate. Place all ingredients in chopper, and chop to a fine texture. Stuff in size 25 cellulose casings, and link at 4-inch intervals. Hold at room temperature for a maximum of 1 hour to dry slightly. Cook in a Jourdan cooker or steam cabinet at 160 to 165 degrees for 15 minutes, or until an internal temperature of 155 degrees is reached. Cold shower and transfer to holding cooler. Peel, package, and hold in cooler at 30 to 34 degrees. This sausage is quite perishable.

LIVER SAUSAGES

Liverwurst varies from soft light pink to darker, firmer sausages. Delicately spiced and seasoned, the smoked varieties are most popular. Liverwurst is rich in iron and vitamins A and B.

Liver Sausage #1

To make this liver sausage, 10 to 20 percent liver, by weight, is added to other cooked meats, such as pork heads, tongues, skin, hearts, and other pieces. Veal or beef can be added and cooked with the pork. Put all pieces of meat in kettle, cover with water, and simmer for 2 to 3 hours until meat can be boned. Do not cook too long or until meat falls from bone. It is important not to over-cook the meat at this stage, or your final product will not be satis-factory. Remove pieces of meat from heat when they can be boned. Cut liver into uniform slices, cover with boiling water, and let sit for about 10 minutes.

Grind all cooked meats with fine grinder plate. Add enough of the liquid in which meats were cooked to make mixture that is soft but not sloppy. It generally takes about one-third as much liquid, by weight, as meat to get proper consistency. Add the fol-lowing for every 10 pounds of cooked mixture.

        6 tbsp. salt
        1 tbsp black pepper
        1 tbsp. sage
  $\frac{1}{4}$ to $\frac{1}{2}$ tsp. red pepper
        2 tsp. allspice

Mix everything together well, then stuff into beef casings. Place in water and simmer about 10 to 30 minutes, until sausage floats. Plunge in cold water, and chill for at least 30 minutes. Hang to dry. Refrigerate. When cooked, sausage may be frozen.

Liver Sausage #2

½ lb. liver	½ lb. salt
15 lbs. pork trimmings	1 oz. sweet marjoram
7½ lbs. lean veal or beef	½ oz. allspice
3½ lbs. dry bread	
10 cups reserved stock from meats	

Cook meats following procedure for Liver Sausage #1, but do not scald liver. Remove bones from meat, and reserve stock. Soak bread in water, squeeze out excess, and add to meat with raw liver. Grind with fine plate. Finely chop onion and garlic, and add with seasonings and 5 pounds of reserved stock. Mix with yours hands or a paddle for about 15 minutes. Stuff into beef casings that have been soaked in warm water. Tie sausages in strings of five or six. Then cook in water not quite boiling. When sausages float, remove and plunge into cold water to cool. Keep in a cool place. They are best fried.

Liverwurst

3 lbs. pork liver	1 tsp. coriander
1 lb. lean pork	1 tsp. marjoram
1 lb. pork belly	1 tsp. ginger
1 cup dark beer	1 tsp. dry mustard
1 tbsp. salt	3 large black olives, sliced

Cut liver and lean pork into ½-inch cubes; dice pork belly. Simmer in beer over medium heat for 50 minutes. Cool overnight in refrigerator. Then grind meats, using fine blade. Add all other ingredients except olives. Form mixture into 18-inch-long, 4-inch-diameter roll, and decorate with olive slices. Wrap in plastic wrap and chill. Makes 4¾ pounds liverwurst.

Soft Liver Sausage

8 lbs. pork liver	5 oz. salt
7 lbs. pork fat	1¼ oz. white pepper
1 small onion, sliced	½ oz. marjoram
8 oz. flour	½ oz. ground pimiento

Remove large veins from liver, cut across, and scald in wire basket to bleach. Cube fat, and place with liver in bowl chopper. Add remaining ingredients, and chop to a smooth paste. Fill into any casings available, natural or synthetic; do no fill too tightly, as casings expand while cooking. Cook in water at 180 degrees for 40 to 60 minutes, depending on size. Keep sausages underwater when cooking. When done, immerse in cold water.

Firm Liver Sausage

2 lbs. pork liver	1 oz. white pepper
8 lbs. fresh pork head meat	1 oz. nutmeg
4 lbs. back fat	⅛ oz. marjoram
1 lb. flour	⅛ oz. ground pimento
4 oz. salt	⅛ oz. lemon thyme

Follow procedure for Soft Liver Sausage, adding head meat to fat before chopping.

Smoked Liver Sausage

2 lbs. pork trimmings	2½ tsp. salt
½ lb. liver	1 tsp. black pepper
¼ tsp. red pepper	½ tsp. allspice
1 cup beef broth	

Cook pork trimmings in water, covered, for 2 hours. Add liver, and cook for another ½ hour. Reserve stock. Remove any bones from trimmings, and grind meats. Add 1 cup of stock, and mix well with seasonings. Stuff in large muslin or beef casings. Smoke for 2 hours at 100 degrees, then simmer until sausage floats. Plunge into cold water, and chill for 30 minutes. Hang to dry.

Smoked Goose Liver Sausage

This is not a pâté de foie gras, but it is delicious.

1 lb. lean pork or poultry meat	½ tsp. white pepper
1 lb. goose liver	¼ tsp. nutmeg
5 tbsp. curing salt	¼ tsp. marjoram
½ cup water	⅛ tsp. ground cloves
½ cup white wine	½ oz. chopped truffles (optional)
1 tsp. salt	

Cup up pork or poultry meat, and place in bowl. Cover with a brine of curing salt, water, and white wine. Refrigerate for 2 days. Grind goose liver and cured pork together. Add remaining ingredients, and mix well. Grind and stuff into muslin casings. Cook in 160-degree water for 1 hour. Cool and dry for 8 hours. Smoke 4 hours at 100 degrees, then chill. Serve cold.

Liverwurst with Bacon

5 lbs. pork liver	1 tsp. cardamom
5 lbs. lean unsmoked bacon	½ tsp. thyme
¼ lb. onions, chopped and blended to a puree	1¼ tsp. mace
2 tsp. white pepper	1 tbsp. saltpeter
¾ tsp. ground ginger	½ cup salt
1 tsp. marjoram	3 tbsp. white corn syrup

Cut liver and bacon into 1- or 2-inch cubes, and blend to a fine puree. Pour mixture into large bowl, add remaining ingredients, and blend well. To stuff casings, use large pastry bag outfitted with No. 6 or larger tube. Slip end of a casing over end of tube, fill bag with meat, and squeeze it into casing, packing it in. When casing is filled to a length of about 12 inches, tie end. Each sausage should weigh about 1½ pounds.

Brunswick Liver Sausage
Braunschweiger Leberwurst

---

20 lbs. fat pork trimmings
    from bellies and heads
2½ lbs. pork or calf ruffle
    (pork fat is preferable)
25 lbs. fresh pork liver
2½ lbs. ham fat trimmings
1 lb. onions

½ lb. braunschweiger
    sausage seasoning
1 lb. salt
  flour
  pickle cure (1 lb. for each
    25 gal. brine)

Run meat and liver through $\frac{5}{64}$-inch plate of meat grinder. Grind as fine as possible, then add remaining ingredients, adding flour as needed for proper consistency. If you prefer, you can mix all ingredients together first, and then run through grinder twice. This sausage must be cut very fine and thoroughly mixed. Use silent cutter if you have one, as it will cut meat the finest. Add ice or ice water while cutting to make mixture very soft.

Stuff into large hog bungs. Before stuffing, take hold of thick end of each hog bung, and draw bung several times through the other hand to remove any moisture from washing and soaking.

When stuffed, tie ends securely, and cook sausage in hot water at 150 to 155 degrees for 30 to 60 minutes, depending on thickness. When cooked, place sausage in cold brine in refrigerator. Use 1 pound pickle cure for each 25 gallons brine. Brine should test 40 degrees by salinometer. Leave in brine for 24 hours. Then hang on sticks to drain in cooler or refrigerator, and they are ready to smoke. Hang in smokehouse and cold smoke. Cool at room temperature, and hang in refrigerator or cooler.

Serdellen Liver Sausage
With Anchovies or Sardines

To make Serdellen Liver Sausage, follow procedure for Brunswick Liver Sausage, but add 3 to 5 percent of the weight in meat of anchovies or sardines, and omit the salt. To make a very fine sardellen sausage, you can use as much as 10 percent anchovies.

To prepare anchovies or sardines, cut off heads and tails, clean out insides of fish, and soak in fresh water for 1 hour to remove some of the salt. Then grind fish as fine as possible, mix with livers, and grind again at the same time livers are ground. Anchovies or sardines should be cut so fine that there is nothing left of them except the taste.

Liver Sausage with Raisins

Follow procedure for Smoked Goose Liver Sausage, but use raisins or currants in the mixture instead of goose livers.

For every 20 pounds of liver sausage, use 1 pound of seedless raisins or dried currants. Wash raisins very clean in two or three changes of boiling water, put into cold water to cool, then add them to sausage mixture. If raisins are large, they can first be cut in two or three pieces or run through $1/4$-inch plate.

Stuff, smoke, and cook sausages in same manner as Smoked Goose Liver Sausage.

Liver and Onion Sausage

30 lbs. pork liver	½ lb. liver sausage
15 lbs. pork back fat	seasoning
7½ lbs. onions	1 lb. salt
	flour

Cut liver into strips from 1 to 2 inches thick, and put into boiling water until cooked through. Then put into ice water. When chilled, grind as fine as possible. Chop onions, and add to liver. Run liver and fat through finest plate of meat grinder, add all other ingredients, and mix well. Stuff into hog bungs or beef middles. Cook as you would other liver sausages.

MISCELLANEOUS SAUSAGES

Salt-Free Salami

1 lb. ground beef	1 tbsp. peppercorns
1 lb. ground pork	½ tsp. liquid smoke
1 cup water	½ tsp. dried minced onion
1 tsp. salt substitute, seasoned	½ tsp. dried minced garlic
or unseasoned	

In medium bowl, thoroughly combine all ingredients. Shape mixture into roll about 3 inches in diameter. Wrap salami in aluminum foil, and refrigerate for 24 hours. Remove foil, and place salami on rack in broiler pan. Bake at 300 degrees for 2 hours. Chill before serving. Keep refrigerated. Makes 10 to 12 servings.

Chicken, Ham, and Tongue Delicacy

50 lbs. lean pork trimmings, cured	cracked ice or ice water
14 lbs. boiled pork tongue, cured	1 lb. frankfurter sage seasoning
16 lbs. ham	2 tbsp. lemon extract
1 16-oz. smoked ham	1 oz. fresh parsley, chopped
6 lbs. chicken	½ lb. sugar
14 lbs. fresh tripe (sinew parts)	flour

Cook chicken until almost cooked through; allow to cool. Cut chicken into ¼-inch cubes, and grind with pork. Cook ham slowly until almost cooked through—about ¾ done. Cool, then cut entire ham and fat into ¼-inch cubes. Cook hog tongues slowly until well cooked. Remove all fat, bone, and skin. Cut into ¼-inch cubes. Chop tripe and pork trimmings, including trimmings from tongue and chicken, as fine as possible through ⁵⁄₆₄-inch plate. Mix all ingredients together thoroughly.

Have a quantity of tin tubes made, 1½ by 6 inches long. Fill prepared meats into tin tubes with hand sausage stuffer, and smooth end with palm of hand. Place tins in hot water at a temperature of 160 degrees for 30 minutes, then allow to cool until they can be handled. Slide meat out of tubes onto clean table, and allow to cool. Chill thoroughly.

Cut dry-cured clear pork fat into ⅛-by-6½-inch slices, and place lengthwise over cooked, cold sausage, covering all sides evenly and covering ends. Do not overhandle.

Slide into weasands, and slip weasand over funnel large enough to admit entire delicacy without disturbing fat. Tie with cord very tightly between individual sausages, forming loop at end. Prick weasands well with a needle, and hang them up.

Place prepared delicacy in colored hot water (170 degrees) for 10 minutes. Rinse off with hot water, then dip into ice-cold water. This will shrink weasand and set fat. Hang to drain and dry, then refrigerate.

Lachs Schinken
Boneless Pork Loins in Beef Bungs

100 lbs. pork loin
     Cure: 8 lbs. salt, 1 lb. pickle cure,
      1 to 2 lbs. sugar, 6 gal. cold water

Cure small boneless loins (3 to 5 pounds) for 18 to 22 days, medium loins (6 to 7 pounds) for 23 to 25 days, and large loins (8 to 10 pounds) for 26 to 30 days. Overhaul on the third, sixth, and tenth days.

When fully cured, remove meat from brine and wipe perfectly dry, then double two together and stuff into beef bung casings. Prick all parts of casing to let air out, and tie tightly with ham cord. Hang in dry refrigerating room with good ventilation. Allow to hang dry for 1 or 2 days. Hang in smokehouse and give them a cold smoke, then place in a dry room again for a day or so.

Lachs Schinken is eaten raw. It is simply sliced and served as is; therefore the meat must be fully cooked and very dry.

Unsmoked Beef Sausage

32½ lbs. beef trimmings, cured	¼ lb. sugar
7½ lbs. plain fresh tripe	½ lb. hamburger seasoning
10 lbs. jowl or back fat	¼ oz. garlic compound
cracked ice or water	½ lb. salt
	flour

Cut tripe into pieces about 1½ inches square. Mix beef, tripe, and all other ingredients except fat. Run mixture through 5/64-inch plate. Add cracked ice or ice water while grinding to cool meat and give good consistency. Put fat through ¼-inch plate, and add to meat mixture. Mix well and stuff into round beef or large sheep casings, making links about 4 inches long. Boil for 15 to 20 minutes, and serve.

Fresh Mixed Sausage

25 lbs. mixed pork, beef, veal, mutton, and lamb waste ends	¼ lb. pork seasoning
	½ lb. salt
cracked ice or ice water	flour

Run mixed meat ends through coarse plate of meat grinder, adding cracked ice or ice water while grinding. Place in tub, add all other ingredients, and mix well. Add water a little at a time until mixture is like paste. Run mixture through finest plate of grinder, and stuff into medium sheep casings. Keep mixture wet enough to make linking easy. This sausage is also good made into patties.

Tomato Pork Sausage

50	lbs. pork trimmings (medium fat)	¼	oz. baking soda
10	lbs. fresh or canned tomatoes	1¼	lbs. salt
½ to 1	lb. sugar	½	lb. pork sausage seasoning
			flour

Prepare tomatoes long enough in advance to let them cool before making sausage, as they must be cold when added to meat. Whether tomatoes are canned or fresh, add sugar and boil for 10 to 15 minutes in their own juice. While boiling, add baking soda to neutralize acid. When cooked, skim all scum, and put boiled tomatoes through sieve to strain out seed, leaving nothing but pulp. Place in bowl and let cool in refrigerator.

Put fresh pork trimmings through ⁵⁄₆₄-inch plate of meat grinder. Place meat in mixer, and add seasonings and flour. Gradually add tomato pulp. Do not add water, as tomatoes contain sufficient moisture. Stuff immediately into medium-wide hog casings, weigh off 1-pound quantities, and link six to the pound. Hang up so that they do not touch each other, and allow to drain thoroughly. Place them in refrigerator.

Cervelat #1

25 lbs. beef trimmings, cured	⅛ lb. thyme
15 lbs. pork trimmings	⅛ lb. basil
10 lbs. pork hearts, cured	¼ lb. sugar
½ lb. cervelat or summer sausage seasoning	flour

Cut fat into small pieces, mix all ingredients, and run through ³⁄₁₆-inch plate of grinder. Place meat in mixer, and blend well. Spread 5 or 6 inches thick on boards, and cover with parchment paper. Place in cooler for 1 to 2 days to cure at 38 to 40 degrees. Remove and mix again to soften meat. Stuff into medium or small beef middles, and hang in a room at 48 to 56 degrees to dry for 4 days. Give sausage a slow smoke for 2 or 3 days, until it takes on a good color. Remove from smokehouse, and place in hot water for 40 to 45 minutes at 155 degrees. Rinse with boiling water and then cold water. Hang at room temperature to dry. The sausage should be kept in cooler until used, to prevent shrinkage.

Cervelat #2

20 lbs. beef trimmings, cured
5 lbs. pork hearts, cured
5 lbs. fat pork jowls, cured
10 lbs. pork cheek meat, cured
10 lbs. pork trimmings, cured

Follow procedure for Cervelat #1.

Cervelat #3

20 lbs. beef trimmings, cured
10 lbs. pork cheek meat, cured
7½ lbs. pork trimmings, cured
7½ lbs. beef hearts, cured
5 lbs. pork fat, cured

Follow procedure for Cervelat #1.

Gotha Cervelat

32½ lbs. lean pork
     trimmings
7½ lbs. beef trimmings,
     cured
½ lb. summer sausage
     seasoning

4 oz. sugar
⅛ lb. thyme
⅛ lb. basil
1½ whole white
     peppercorns

Carefully trim all sinews. Cut back fat into ¼-inch cubes. Chop meat in chopper—first beef, then pork, and then fat. Chop very fine. After chopper has made two revolutions, add remaining ingredients, adding peppercorns last, and continue chopping until meat is cut fine. Spread mixture 5 to 6 inches thick on boards, and cover with parchment paper. Place in cooler at 38 to 40 degrees, and let it remain for 2 days. Then remove from cooler, and mix by hand just until pliable. Stuff into hog bungs about 20 inches long. Hand in cold drying room for 2 weeks at 40 to 45 degrees. The third week, increase temperature to 48 to 56 degrees, and keep for a few more days. Hang in smokehouse in a cool smoke for 3 days and nights. After sausage is smoked, hang in a dry room at 45 to 55 degrees, and keep there a couple of weeks until medium dry.

Fat Pork Thuringian Mettwurst

50 lbs. fat pork trimmings, cured	¼ oz. whole mustard seed
½ lb. mettwurst seasoning	¼ lb. sugar
	flour

Run pork trimmings through ¼-inch hole, and all other meats through ⁵/₆₄-inch hole. Place meats and all remaining ingredients in mixer or mix by hand. When well mixed, stuff mixture into beef rounds. Tie in 1-pound rings, leaving 1 inch of twine between ends to hang on sausage sticks. Hang in smokehouse and give a cool slow smoke for about 36 hours, or until they have a nice brown appearance. Smoke sausage as soon as it is stuffed.

This sausage must have plenty of fat. Do not trim any fat off meats. Use medium fat trimmings. If meat used in this sausage is too lean, color will be a dark red and will not have the correct appearance of mettwurst.

Thuringian Mettwurst with Beef

40 lbs. pork trimmings, cured	¼ oz. whole mustard seed
10 lbs. beef trimmings, cured	¼ lb. sugar
½ lb. mettwurst seasoning	flour

Follow procedure for Fat Pork Thuringian Mettwurst.

Thuringian Mettwurst

---

25 lbs. pork trimmings,
cured
7½ lbs. fat pork trimmings,
cured
10 lbs. hog cheek meat, cured
5 lbs. plain tripe

½ lb. mettwurst
seasoning
¼ oz. whole mustard seed
¼ lb. sugar
flour

Follow procedure for Fat Pork Thuringian Mettwurst.

Thuringian Mettwurst with Mutton

7½ lbs. beef trimmings,
cured
5 lbs. tongue or neck
trimmings, cured
12½ lb. fat pork trimmings,
cured
15 lbs. mutton trimmings,
cured

10 lb. plain tripe
½ lb. mettwurst seasoning
¼ oz. whole mustard seed
¼ lb. sugar
flour

Follow procedure for Fat Pork Thuringian Mettwurst.

Landjaeger Sausage
Hunter's Sausage

30 lbs. lean beef, cured
20 lbs. fat pork trimmings,
    cured
 4 oz. sugar
½ lb. summer sausage
    seasoning

¾ oz. powdered caraway
    seeds
½ oz. garlic powder
    flour

Run meats through ⅛-inch plate of grinder. Place in mixer or mix by hand, adding remaining ingredients. Mix well together, then stuff into hog casings loosely, about half full. Form links 5 to 6 inches long, separating meat so that there is about ½ inch of casing empty at ends of each link. Cut off in double links, then lap empty ends of sausage casing over to close.

Lay sausages on board, insert small, square stick between each pair of links, then lay another board on top of sausages and put a weight on it to press sausages flat. Place all in cooler at about 38 to 40 degrees for 3 to 4 days. This allows meat to cure and makes sausages set. Then remove boards from cooler, take sausages off, and hang them on rods to put in smokehouse. Give them a cold, slow smoke for 24 hours.

Cooked Salami

25 lbs. boneless lean chuck or other lean beef, cured	1/2 oz. garlic compound
	1/2 lb. sausage seasoning
15 lbs. pork trimmings, cured	1/2 oz. brandy flavor flour
10 lbs. firm pork back fat, cured	

Put beef and fat through 3/16-inch plate, and pork through 1/4-inch hole. Put all meat into mixer, add remaining ingredients, and mix well. Spread mixture 6 to 7 inches deep on tray or shelf in cooler, and hold at 38 to 40 degrees for 24 hours.

Stuff into sheep bungs about 2 1/2 inches in diameter, wrapping with twine or not, as desired. Hang sausage in cooler for a day or two to develop color. Place in water at 150 degrees, and cook for 2 to 3 hours, depending on thickness. After cooking, hang them in smokehouse and give them a cold smoke for 20 to 24 hours. Remove from smokehouse, and hang in a dry room until ready to use.

Smoked Pepperoni

The traditional Italian-style pepperoni is not smoked; smoke-flavored pepperoni is considered objectionable in the Italian trade.

22½	lbs. regular pork trimmings	6	oz. sweet paprika
15	lbs. beef chuck	3	oz. decorticated ground
7½	lbs. pork hearts		pepper
5	lbs. pork cheeks	2	oz. capsaicin
1 lb., 9	oz. salt	2	oz. whole fennel seed
½	lb. sugar	½	oz. sodium nitrate

Grind meats through ½-inch plate and then through ⅛-inch plate. Add remaining ingredients, and mix for 5 minutes or until well blended. Stuff into 48- to 44-millimeter natural casings or, if for slicing, No. 1 x 32 fibrous casings. Hold for 9 to 11 days at 38 degrees. Transfer to a green room maintained at 65 degrees and 69 percent humidity, and hold for 48 hours. Smoke for 60 hours at 90 degrees, and dry smoke until red color develops. Then adjust relative humidity to 80 percent and finish smoking. Hold for 21 days in a drying room at 53 degrees and 69 percent humidity. Shrinkage is about 35 percent.